HACK THE TIME WEALTH MATRIX

HACK
——— THE ———
TIME-WEALTH MATRIX

CREATING REAL WEALTH

IN A WORLD OF FAKE MONEY

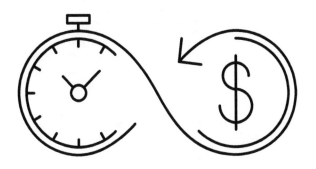

PAT "ROCK" DAY

HOUNDSTOOTH
PRESS

HACK THE TIME WEALTH MATRIX

Creating Real Wealth in a World of Fake Money

FIRST EDITION

ISBN   978-1-5445-4582-0   *Hardcover*

978-1-5445-4581-3   *Paperback*

978-1-5445-4583-7   *Ebook*

To Mom and Dad—I did not realize how little Time we had—
thank you for the wealth I am just now understanding.

To Janet—Time is rushing by—my last Epoch is yours to spend.

To Ryan and Russell—I love the Time we spend
together—do not waste Time on me.

To Oliver and Beckett—your Time is in the future—this story is
really for you, and I hope you pull it from the shelf one day and smile,
thinking about Rock and Cookie and Saturday morning cartoons.

CONTENTS

INTRODUCTION 9

PART ONE: PREPARING

1. WEALTH ISN'T WHAT YOU THINK IT IS 15
2. TIME ISN'T WHAT YOU THINK IT IS 33
3. MONEY ISN'T WHAT YOU THINK IT IS 41
4. INVESTING ISN'T WHAT YOU THINK IT IS 61
5. THE MONEY MATRIX ISN'T WHAT YOU THINK IS 87

PART TWO: EXECUTION

6. PUTTING THE PIECES TOGETHER 109
7. EPOCH I: LEARNING AND BASE-BUILDING—
   BIRTH TO AGE THIRTY-THREE 115
8. EPOCH II: PROTECTION AND ACCUMULATION—
   AGE THIRTY-THREE TO AGE SIXTY-SIX 135
9. EPOCH III: WITHDRAWING/PASSING TIME—
   AGE SIXTY-SIX TO AGE NINETY-NINE 197
10. MENTAL MODELS, OR HOW TO THINK ABOUT TIME 217
11. BUILDING LINES TO CONQUER TIME 231
12. CLOSING THE BOOKS 255

APPENDIX 259
SAVINGS APPENDIX 263
ACKNOWLEDGMENTS 269
NOTES 271

INTRODUCTION

Time is your most valuable asset.

Understanding, mastering, sharing, and investing time will create real wealth for you and your family. Unfortunately, most of us dabble around the edges of time without considering its impact on our lives.

What qualifies me to write on this topic is that over the last thirty years, I have helped thousands of people from ages 18 to 103 manage their financial lives. I've watched over clients' shoulders as children were born, educated, and sent on their way. I've been there as clients begin retirement, enjoy life, and eventually succumb as time and mortality take their natural course.

During the time shared with all these folks, I have seen how the culmination of all their life choices has shaped each one's life era, which is painted on top of an ever-changing canvas of economic, social, and technological change.

I've learned that we each have a multidimensional "matrix" of intersecting emotional, physical, and ephemeral experiences that shape our decision-making processes and drive good and bad results. Do I eat in or take out, buy a lottery ticket, run the red light, ask someone on a first date, invest in stocks, take a new job offer, move to a new city, buy a home, or get married?

We consciously or subconsciously plot every decision on this matrix, considering the risk and potential cost of saying yes or no. Some decisions are of little consequence: eating in or taking out. Others, though, change the direction of our lives, things like moving to a new city or getting married.

Hacking this matrix means understanding how our mind handles information to generate a response. We then need to take stock of how our experiences shape our attitudes toward who and what we prioritize, along with our perceptions of risk. This inside information will allow us to make better choices as we move through life.

Over time, I've also watched what I call fake money damage financial futures in two ways. The first type of fake money is the paper currency in a wallet or savings account that is steadily worth less each year because of inflation. This relentless destruction of value gradually robs us of our wealth and the time we worked to earn it. The other, more insidious, type of fake money is an influencer-inspired lifestyle. Little-used purchases that one feels are needed to complete the lifestyle are acquired, but once acquired, they are of little use.

On the flip side, I have also witnessed how real wealth, financial and nonfinancial, affects people and their families. Things like family and friends, a calling, and understanding what is truly important in life significantly improved clients' lives. My front-row seat as an advisor has allowed me to see why real wealth unquestionably means the things that last and then undoubtedly outlast us.

My advisor role has also given me the unique gift of traveling alongside my clients as they face the three Epochs of Wealth: the Learning Epoch, the Accumulation Epoch, and the

Withdrawing/Passing Epoch. I have been along for the entire journey with some; others, I joined somewhere along the path.

Using all this experience, I'll begin by guiding you through rethinking wealth, time, risk, and the future. We'll then walk through the three epochs, clarifying a few milestones and what to expect as you travel along the trail. I will also provide a shortcut to measuring the time and distance to reach your destination. Finally, we will close with tools to help you engage with the future. Each part builds on the previous parts, so it's best to work through the chapters in order.

An important aside, while I describe what investments are, I do not go into depth on this topic. There are thousands of books on stocks, bonds, and asset allocation. This book is about better understanding how money and investments fit into your life. Also, while my orientation and cultural references are distinctly American, the ideas about risk, time, and wealth are universal. Still, I apologize if some jokes don't make sense.

The Wealth Equation I've created is a formula that clarifies how to balance different parts of our lives. I'll describe and return to this equation throughout.

When we are done with our time together, you will be able to:

- Look at wealth differently.
- Think about time in new ways.
- Understand that compounding time and knowing what is valuable to you is the antidote to fake money.

Equally important, you will see how the different complex parts of life interact, what money and wealth can be, and ideally, have a roadmap to find your reason for getting out of bed in the morning.

I hope you enjoy the journey!

PART ONE

PREPARING

It's a warm spring evening, and I am seated among my friends in a nondescript bar in Cabo Sans Lucas. We listen intently to our guide, a former Navy Seal, as he drinks his piña colada and gives us the rundown of our upcoming adventure: racing across the Baja Peninsula in high-performance Baja Challenge cars.

He laid out the essentials—spacing, radios, safety gear. But his last words still linger: "Gentlemen, this isn't Disney World. No rails here to keep you on the track."

We all knew where the gas and brake pedals were and could have just hopped in the cars and taken off. However, taking the time to have the complete picture of what the cars could do, how they did it, and things to watch out for on the road increased the odds of a successful trip.

Similarly, understanding all the variables of wealth and how to feather the clutch on them when needed is paramount to not only just crossing the finish line but successfully crossing it in a time, place, and style of your own choosing.

Consider Part One as your predeparture briefing.

"It ain't what you don't know that gets you into trouble. It's what you know for sure that just ain't so."

—MARK TWAIN

CHAPTER 1

WEALTH ISN'T WHAT YOU THINK IT IS

DEFINING WEALTH

Wealth has multiple definitions.

The first is what you probably think it is: a great quantity or store of money, valuable possessions, property, or other riches: the wealth of a city.

Other definitions include words like abundance, monetary, being rich, or affluent.

The most interesting to me is the last entry, which is no longer in use—Obsolete. happiness.[1]

Bummer! I thought the whole reason to accumulate wealth was to increase happiness!

Society can easily catalog most of the things it classifies as wealth. Assets, liabilities, and net worth are topics covered in the financial press, television, and bestsellers. But in reality, financial assets are just one form of wealth.

Other forms of wealth, which are not easily quantified or

accounted for, offer nonfinancial benefits, provide support, and can be just as fulfilling as accumulating financial assets.

To be clear, my goal is to guide you toward wealth. It just might be different from the type that gets splashy headlines in magazines like *Forbes* or *Money*. These forms of nonfinancial wealth serve alongside financial wealth as the foundation for a more holistic prosperity.

Adding these variables together equals wealth, and everyone has a personal Wealth Equation that they calculate:

$$\text{Wealth} = FF + EKW + J + S + FA + T$$

What are these variables that make up the Wealth Equation?

FAMILY AND FRIENDS—STRONG CONNECTIONS PROVIDE A SENSE OF BELONGING

(Wealth = **Family and Friends** + EKW + J + S + FA + T)

Citizen Kane is Orson Welles's thought-provoking film from the 1940s that delves into the fictional life of Charles Kane, a charismatic and ambitious individual with a dark past. The film follows him from childhood through the mercilessly achieved pinnacles of wealth and success as a media tycoon all the way to his final day.

In the memorable opening scene where, alone in his mansion, surrounded by material possessions but devoid of genuine human connections, Kane utters his last word, "Rosebud." As the movie wraps up, we see Kane's lifetime of collected treasures tossed onto a fire, including the most valuable one, his childhood sled named Rosebud—a potent symbol of the happiest phase of his life. Welles masterfully shows how a life filled with riches and prestige can feel empty without meaningful personal relationships.

What Orson Welles knew instinctively is what science has proven. Family and friends are vital to growing up and growing old in a successful manner.

Family. Only a few people have known you (and that you have known) for your whole life, your immediate family: mom, dad, brothers, sisters, sons, daughters, or some combination of this mix. Keep them close because they are family. Also, selfishly, it is essential to keep these people close because they will likely be the ones taking care of us when needed. Research suggests that 75 percent of us will need some help in our later years, and it is these family members who are typically providing this care.[2]

I've personally observed a transition where clients, advancing into their later years, are sharing responsibilities with their children. These children, still in their fifties yet lovingly referred to as "the kids," are progressively shouldering more day-to-day responsibilities, easing the load on my clients.

Besides our immediate families, we often consider friends the family we choose for ourselves. As we march through life, building and maintaining close social ties is critical to our well-being. Research suggests that friends help boost happiness, reduce stress, and improve self-confidence. Equally important, they are there in the times of crisis we will experience through our lives: the death of a loved one, illnesses, and job loss.[3]

Researchers have also found that social networks are as important as workouts. Using Fitbits, surveys, and self-assessments, these researchers determined strong social networks significantly improved stress, happiness, and positivity over just the number of steps in a day or the resting heart rate.[4]

So being fit is great. Being fit together with family and friends is even better!

It is clear cherishing your family and friends matters, but placing a high value on your best friends is an even better way to increase the odds of living your best life.

Studies indicate we tend to prune the more superficial relationships as we age, leaving us with fewer but deeper friendships that make us happy.[5]

Nurturing these close relationships with family and friends is vital if you're aiming for a life that's not just long but also filled with health and happiness.

This form of nonfinancial wealth is not easily put on a balance sheet.

"Instead of viewing the time we spend with friends and family as luxuries, we can see that these relationships are among the most powerful determinants of our well-being and survival."

—DEAN ORNISH

EXPERIENCES—ACHIEVEMENTS, FAILURES, AND ADVENTURES BUILD A FOUNDATION

(Wealth = FF + **Experience** KW + J + S + FA + T)

From the time we burn our finger on a hot stove as a toddler, our lives are simply a collection of experiences that help us navigate the next adventure. We can read a book on how to ride a bike, but we need to get on it to learn how to ride it.

Experiential learning starts with parents telling toddlers not to touch the stove because it is hot. They touch it anyway, once.

Later on, parents run alongside the child's bike to get it moving fast enough for the child to catch their balance. Finally, at some point, they let go to see their child ride on their own.

Each experience a parent provides is another step in preparing the child for a future without them.

We sometimes stumble and trip as we grow up. We occasionally burn our fingers, take spills off our bikes, fail assignments, and become involved in dangerous situations. Interestingly enough, all these experiences teach us more than if we had just sailed through a problem without a hitch the first time.

Thomas Edison is famous for saying, "I have not failed. I've just found ten thousand ways that won't work."

Akin to Edison, another person whose life is full of experiences is Elon Musk. Musk's journey is nothing short of remarkable, and his setbacks are as well-known as his successes. Like Edison learning from failed experiments, every rocket ship Elon blows up is another lesson learned.

His wealth of experience has led him to use reusable parts in his rockets. This innovation helped him crack the code to make space travel more affordable.

In their own words:

I messed up the first three launches. The first three launches failed. And fortunately the fourth launch, which was, that was the last money that we had for Falcon 1. That fourth launch worked. Or it would have been—that would have been it for SpaceX. But fate liked us that day. So, the fourth launch worked.[6]

Experience is a building block in the foundation that leads to the next level, but only if we learn from our experiences. John Dewey, an influential thinker from the early twentieth century, postulated that while all real education came through experience, not all experiences were equally educational.

Learning from experiences means reflecting on them and incorporating them into our lives. From Edison's thousands of "failures" to Musk's launches, each experience taught them something. So, how do you learn from experience?

The experiential-learning theory tells us that a cycle of experiencing, reflecting, thinking, and acting is how we best learn from our experiences.[7]

Building on our successes and failures and tracking them in some fashion will allow us to lean on our experiences when needed.

When we think about Edison and Musk, two influential figures from different time periods, do we admire the wealth they accumulated or their revolutionary accomplishments?

The light bulb, the movie camera, the alkaline battery, Tesla, Star Link, and SpaceX are more than just inventions. They're time-, energy-, and money-savers that have enhanced all our lives.

Every day, we enter the world armed with a blend of our life experiences. These experiences have a unique way of enhancing and simplifying our lives.

Like relationships, this asset is hard to account for on a balance sheet but is an important source of our wealth.

"Learn as though you will live forever. Live as though you will die tomorrow."

—John Wooden

KNOWLEDGE AND WISDOM—WHAT
YOU KNOW AND HOW TO USE IT

(Wealth = FF + E **Knowledge Wisdom** + J + S + FA + T)

In building his resume of experiences, the twenty-two-year-old George Washington lost his first battle to the French as a young officer at Fort Necessity near Pittsburgh. Historians say his signature on the surrender document helped fuel the tensions that led to the French and Indian War, then a global war between France and England, and finally, the American Revolution.

As we all know, Washington did not let that loss derail his future. In the subsequent years of his life, Washington learned valuable lessons from the British Army and combined these with his knowledge of the North American terrain, gained from his time as a young surveyor. This blend of formal military understanding and personal experience enabled him to lead a remarkable victory over the British in the War of Independence.

These days, our formal education comes from high school or college rather than surveying the frontier or the British Army. But just as with Washington, it's the blend of this structured learning and our own experiences that helps us identify our strengths and craft our unique sets of talents.

Scott Adams introduced the concept of a "talent stack," in his book How to Fail at Almost Everything and Still Win Big. It is a mix of all the things you enjoy and excel at, making you truly stand out.

In their own words:

In my case, I can draw better than most people, but I'm hardly an artist. And I'm not any funnier than the average standup comedian who never makes it big, but I'm funnier than most people. The magic is that few people can draw well and write jokes. It's the combination of the two that makes what I do so rare. And when you add in my business background, suddenly I had a topic that few cartoonists could hope to understand without living it.[8]

In the world of work, a talent stack, or knowledge, are the things that are taught and the things you learn on your own.

Wisdom is a horse of a different color. It's the ability to combine this knowledge and experience into a coherent strategy to improve your own life and the lives of those around you successfully.

Abraham Lincoln's use and timing of the Emancipation Proclamation exemplify this type of wisdom. Lincoln used all his life skills from his frontier childhood of log-rolling and house raisings with folks from all classes to reading Shakespeare, Blackstone's Commentaries, and learning Euclidian geometry.

Lincoln issued the Proclamation as the tide of the war moved in the Union's direction and reframed the Civil War, making it a war for the abolition of slavery. This reframe made it politically and morally difficult for European nations, particularly Britain, which had strong antislavery sentiments, to support the Confederacy.

Like Lincoln, the combination of all your experiences and knowledge with the superglue of wisdom is a very valuable package, one that others might find useful and be willing to pay for over time.

Although challenging to measure, this type of wealth will

ultimately manifest in your financial statements through increased income and assets. Equally significant, grasping the foundations of your actions paves the way for a happier life.

"Knowledge comes from learning. Wisdom comes from living."
—Anthony Douglas Williams

WORK—A JOB, A CAREER, OR A CALLING

(Wealth = FF + EKW + **JOB** + S + FA + T)

A study on the work orientations of physicians, nurses, educators, programmers, and clerical staff unexpectedly revealed that regardless of position or income, people are pretty evenly divided about how they view work.[9]

The findings? If there were thirty employees in a similar role, statistically, they would fall equally into one of the following work orientations:

Job—Ten would say they prefer jobs that do not interfere with their personal lives. Work is a means to an end.

Career—Ten would say they want steadily increasing responsibility, raises, and titles. They are looking for a defined path forward, along with social recognition.

Calling—Ten would say their work is integral to their identity. Work for these individuals provides personal fulfillment and satisfaction. Individuals with this orientation will likely say they would do their jobs even if they were not paid.

These findings remain relevant regardless of income or job duties, e.g., doctor versus clerical staff. Equally important, the authors did not make a value judgment on which orientation is better. They determined it was just how people fit work into their own lives.

Understanding how we internalize work and its place in our lives is vital to solving the Wealth Equation. If work is a calling, it may crowd out other forms of wealth but leave one happy with the decision to prioritize it over other material things. Ensuring that our work does not crowd out different, more important parts of our lives is vital if this work is just a job. Understanding the difference is crucial.

The book So Good They Can't Ignore You: Why Skills Trump Passion in the Quest for Work You Love argues that trying to discover your calling and then finding the work you love is backward.[10] The book expands on Adams's talent stack by indicating that building skills or talents moves one toward a calling. Put another way, a job morphs into a career that leads to a calling.

Discovering our work orientation is the key takeaway: two people might work side by side for decades, but while one finds a calling in their work, the other might see it as just a job.

It is crucial to understand our work orientations since work takes up a significant chunk of our lives. Then defining our relationship with work helps us better comprehend how we see ourselves and the value we place on what we do.

This form of wealth is internal and, like other things, not easily put into dollars, but it is wealth most still need to attain.

"Money is a neutral indicator of value. By aiming to make money, you're aiming to be valuable."

—Cal Newport

STUFF—THERE IS STUFF WE
MUST HAVE, OR IS THERE?

(Wealth = FF + EKW + J + **STUFF** + FA + T)

Consumers never had a chance.

Statista.com reports that total advertising expenditures in North America in 2021 were over $300 billion.[11] Over time, advertisers have spent enormous sums of money to get us to buy stuff we both need and don't need.

It is not just the money advertisers spend but how effectively they deploy it.

Advertisers have turned to academics, who have determined not only what we buy but why. This study of why we buy has led to a theory of consumer behavior called the Diderot effect.

To understand this, we need to rewind to the 1760s and a man named Denis Diderot. Diderot's receipt of a small fortune from Empress Catherine the Great of Russia led to a great deal of regret on Diderot's part.

Diderot wrote an essay entitled *Regrets for My Old Dressing Gown, or a Warning to Those Who Have More Taste Than Fortune*, Diderot narrates how his simple purchase of a red robe spiraled into an overhaul of his possessions to align with his newfound wealth and altered self-image.[12] This red robe served as more than just clothing; it was the catalyst that triggered a cascade of changes, from new chairs to art, all in pursuit of a lifestyle that matched the robe's elegance. Ironically, this pursuit of harmony in his surroundings led to a mismatch with his financial reality, culminating in luxury laced with debt.

In their own words:

But that's not all, my friend. Lend an ear to the ravages of luxury, the results of a consistent luxury.

My old robe was one with the other rags that surrounded me. A straw chair, a wooden table, a rug from Bergamo, a wood plank that held up a few books, a few smoky prints without frames, hung by its corners on that tapestry. Between these prints, three or four suspended plasters formed, along with my old robe, the most harmonious indigence.

All is now discordant. No more coordination, no more unity, no beauty.[13]

This tendency to buy complementary items to go along with a new purchase has come to be called the Diderot effect. The book Culture and Consumption explains the Diderot effect. The book suggests purchases are tied more closely to identity than practicality.[14] It also points out that the first purchase leads to a series of acquisitions. You need new shirts and slacks to go with your new jacket.

IKEA has mastered this art by grouping lifestyle objects in display rooms and catalogs.

Buying a bed? Well, here is a dresser that goes with it, along with this cute carpet you need to complete the theme.

Apple has created whole ecosystems of complementary products. Have an iPhone? Just buy an iPad, and you can Airdrop data between them. Oh, and if your friends have Apple products, you can iMessage!

Advertising works, so it is no wonder everyone wants a new BMW to drive to Starbucks, where they will show off their designer threads. Seldom will people talk about driving their Fiesta with their Folgers to show off their Kirkland fashion.

Diderot experienced overwhelming buyer's remorse and would have strongly urged his younger self to part with the red robe rather than gain an entirely new environment. Similarly, consider the counsel your wiser, older self might offer when pondering a new purchase.

It is easy to value and put houses, cars, watches, golf clubs, computers, and TVs on a balance sheet. Knowing their value is helpful.

However, there is more value in knowing why you own these things, so they do not control you.

"Stuff is not passive. Stuff wants your time, attention, allegiance. But you know it as well as I do, life is more important than the things we accumulate."

—DAVE BRUNO

FINANCIAL ASSETS—HAVING ENOUGH TO THRIVE

(Wealth = FF + EKW + J + S + **Financial Assets** + T)

More dollars are better. Really?

The problems that go along with accumulating dollars cross the centuries, from Midas in the eighth century to Notorious B.I.G. in our current generation, who raps about how the more money he has the more problems he has.

This begs a question: if more money brings more happiness, why are there so many stories of multimillion-dollar lottery winners declaring bankruptcy and rap stars singing about their problems?

The flip side of the coin comprises stories of people with practically nothing who share what little they have with strangers.

In "Science Behind Behavior," Utpal Dholakia narrates a heartfelt anecdote from his high school years involving an Indian village woman. Despite her limited means, she opened her heart and home, offering him tea and food. On a relative scale, this act of kindness, coming from someone living with so little, represented an unparalleled level of generosity.[15]

Turns out that dollars, stocks, bonds, gold, Bitcoin, and any other form of money are just things like watches and cars. Much as Diderot and various lottery winners found out after receiving their fortunes, it was enough until it wasn't, and a young student found that a little is enough to share with a stranger.

It is our relationship with money that determines if we have enough.

Financial assets are easy to put on the balance sheet. While it may take time to accumulate, they have a clearly defined value. However, how many commas we need in the tally of our net worth is more a function of understanding what we value over what we want.

Knowing both the quantity and quality of our financial assets is a great source of wealth.

"For what will it profit a man if he gains the whole world and forfeits his soul?"

—MATTHEW 16:26

TIME—THE SOURCE OF ALL WEALTH

(Wealth = FF + EKW + J + S + FA + **Time**)

All wealth requires the expenditure of Time to acquire it. Therefore, no wealth exists without Time.

Building a strong family and strong friendships requires you to be present in people's lives. Experiences, knowledge, and wisdom require you to spend Time experiencing, going to school, and applying what you learn. For a job, career, or calling, it takes Time to learn skills that are of value to society. Acquiring material things requires Time to build them or to accumulate money to purchase them.

Time, therefore, is the most important part of the Wealth Equation. It is a silent partner in everything we acquire.

Regrettably, Time is a linearly depleting asset, like a gold mine that is eventually played out. We use every second, minute, hour, day, and year that passes, and that Time cannot be used again. Like air, we do not value it until we are about to run out of it.

Fortunately, we have discovered a method to store Time for later use.

The Wealth Equation allows us to store Time in our other forms of wealth to spend later or pass on to others.

$$\text{Wealth} = FF + EKW + J + S + FA + T$$

where:
FF = Friends and Family
EKW = Experience, Knowledge, Wisdom
J = Job, Career, Calling
S = Stuff
FA = Financial Assets
T = Time

This means that while Time is a linearly depleting asset that goes to zero, our other assets can compound. This means if we effectively manage Time, our wealth can be larger than the Time we were given at birth.

Just a heads up, I capitalize the word "Time" at various points throughout this work. While this may deviate from standard grammatical conventions, there will be points that I want to remind you of the importance of this depleting asset. The rationale for this will become more apparent as you continue reading. I hope.

"Time stays long enough for anyone who will use it."

—LEONARDO DA VINCI

TAKEAWAYS

If asked how wealthy they are, most people's answers would likely be approximations of their balance sheet net worth. Something like, "I am worth $1 million."

It is doubtful you would get an answer that sounds like this:

I've just come back from spending a weekend with the kids and grandkids. We played games and watched *Kung Fu Panda* together. While we were there, one of my son's friends, who is interested in my field, asked for my thoughts, and I provided some red flags to look out for in companies in our space. On the ride home, we discussed the future, and while the car might only last a few more years, our retirement accounts should be able to support us for the next twenty-five years; God willing, we have that long. All in all, I think we are wealthy enough.

Like the perfect perfume scent or your favorite pair of jeans, we personalize the Wealth Equation to each individual. It is some combination of the important variables that make us who we are and determine how we will look back on our time here on Earth.

As we will discover in the following chapters, Time is the top ingredient in accumulating wealth. Let's examine how we interact with time and how our relationship with time has changed over the last century.

CHAPTER 2

TIME ISN'T WHAT YOU THINK IT IS

DEFINING TIME

Everyone is given the same gift by their parents on the day they are born. It is not driven by class, race, income, or any other characteristics except the fact you are suddenly here.

We are given one lifetime, which is the gift of Time.

At the instant this Time is given, it begins to disappear. Some of us will make life choices that add or subtract a few years. Some will be blessed with strong genes and a long life, while others, the most heartbreaking stories told, will be short. However long or short, it is ours to make the most of.

It is both a blessing and a curse that we are not told how much Time we are given.

ROCK'S MUSINGS

We must acknowledge that family income, ancestry, and birthplace can influence the length of our lives. However, we must empower ourselves and seize the time we've been given to make a difference. Some of us face higher obstacles, but that doesn't mean we cannot be the exception—the ones who overcome challenges.

In your own home, take inspiration from individuals like William Kamkwamba, a Malawian inventor and author, who, at fourteen, built a windmill to provide electricity for his village, becoming a symbol of sustainable energy solutions.

In your community, follow the lead of Marley Dias, who initiated the #1000BlackGirlBooks campaign, promoting diversity in literature by collecting and donating thousands of books featuring black female protagonists to schools and libraries.

And in the world, let the courage of Malala Yousafzai inspire you. A brave advocate for girls' education, she began activism at a young age, even surviving a near-fatal attack by the Taliban at fifteen. Her relentless fight for education rights made her the youngest Nobel Peace Prize laureate at seventeen.

Remember, while we will later explore systems to help in this book, you can be the agent of change. Embrace your potential to make a positive impact, both locally and globally. You can help create a brighter and more equal future.

TIME—THE ASSET THAT CONTROLS ALL WEALTH

This blessing/curse is the way it has always been since the dawn of time.

It is amazing to think we have been around for over 200,000 years. And while time does not speed up or slow down, it's interesting how our interaction with time has evolved over the past century.

For most of the recorded time, having a little land allowed you to survive. Having a lot of land allowed you to become wealthy. But nature controlled what the land could produce, and it took its own sweet time.

THE FARMER—SUNRISE TO SUNSET, SEVEN DAYS A WEEK

In 1860, 80 percent of people in the United States were rural, and farmers comprised 59 percent of the labor force.[16] Only six million people lived in cities.[17]

A farmer wakes up with his family at dawn and works until sunset. A farmer's skill, knowledge, and experience tell them when to plant the crops in the spring and harvest in the fall. The cows are milked two times daily, and eggs are collected once daily. The sun, the seasons, and the calendar set the rhythm of life. Generations still pass farms, knowledge, and a little wisdom to each other.

If you asked a farmer in 1860 what time it was, they might look at the field of corn and say it was about time to harvest.

THE BAKER AND THE BLACKSMITH—IT TAKES AS LONG AS IT TAKES, NINE TO NINE, SIX DAYS A WEEK

Alongside the farmer, the baker and the blacksmith provided their services to the population. These and other artisans worked long hours. Like the land the farmers owned and managed, these artisans owned the tools of their production. They were in control of the product from beginning to end. Their knowledge and experience let them know the best metal for the job or when the dough had risen sufficiently to put in the oven. Once they started a process, they had to see it through to the end.

If you inquired about the time in 1860, one of them might respond, "It's time to cast the metal or proof the dough."

THE BANKER AND THE RAILROAD—WORKING BANKER'S HOURS NINE TO FIVE, FIVE DAYS A WEEK

In one lifetime, the world changed.

By 1920, less than half the US population was rural, and farmers made up just 27 percent of the labor force.[18] In the span of just sixty years, approximately fifty-three million people had moved to cities.[19]

Additionally, the banking system, which had endured numerous crises, including the 1907 global panic, began to be reformed. The Federal Reserve was established in 1913 to propel the country forward. In 1933, Congress enacted laws to curb bank speculation and to create the Federal Deposit Insurance Corporation, which began operation in 1934. As a result, people began to have confidence in the banking system.

This was the start of the world we currently live in.

But the shift from farming to industry, and the revolution in transport and communications that began with the steam engine and the telegraph, have fundamentally reshaped our perceptions of time and wealth.

If you were riding a horse from the Atlantic to the Pacific, the specific time of noon wouldn't matter to you. You'd consider it noon when the sun was directly overhead. Now, imagine multiple trains on the same tracks, traveling in opposite directions. Suddenly, the exact moment of noon becomes incredibly crucial!

The railroads forced us to adopt a schedule of four time zones across the United States, and this became law with the Standard Time Act of 1918.[20] This conformity allowed for organized shipping schedules across the country that benefited both the railways and industry.

It also allowed industry to control the work schedules of the fifty-three million people living in cities.

THE CLOCK—TAKE THE 8:15 INTO THE CITY

We've transitioned from a preindustrial lifestyle shaped by the natural rhythms of the seasons to a postindustrial era dictated by the ticking of a clock.

The factory system brought about the specialization of labor, boosting productivity. However, it also changed how individuals experience their daily lives. Most workers lost control over the final products of their labor. No longer did a person grow their food or forge a piece of equipment. Instead, they built a component that contributed to a larger, more complex product desired by others.

In this system, it's overwhelmingly the owners who amass wealth. Their employees earn paychecks, but they only sometimes get satisfaction from their work. For those who have not found their calling, punching the Time clock has become the controlling force in life, and we have adapted to its relentless rhythm.

In our current era, understanding how to master the clock and the calendar is vital to accumulating wealth, so we, like farmers, craftsmen, and business owners, can amass wealth and control our future.

"Capitalism figured out how to conquer nature."

—Dr. Ben Sawyer

EVERYONE RECEIVES TIME, BUT NO ONE HAS THE SAME AMOUNT

While it is a fact that everyone is granted the gift of Time when they are born, each individual approaches this gift in their own distinct manner.

Some take Time for granted because it is always there. Others are diligent and take advantage of their Time. Aesop's fable "The Ant and the Grasshopper" sets this discussion up:

> One bright day in late autumn, a family of ants were bustling about in the warm sunshine, drying out the grain they had stored up during the summer, when a starving grasshopper, his fiddle under his arm, came up and humbly begged for a bite to eat. "What!" cried the ants in surprise, "haven't you stored anything away for the winter? What in the world were you doing all last summer?" "I didn't have time to store up any food," whined the grasshopper. "I was so busy making music that before I knew it the summer was gone." The ants shrugged their shoulders in disgust. "Making music, were you?" they cried. "Very well; now dance!" And they turned their backs on the grasshopper and went on with their work.

The moral of the story is obvious to all: the grasshopper should not have frittered away his Time at parties and should have focused on putting something away for the hard times ahead. This is as true today as it was when this story was told to little Greek children in ancient times.

But in today's reading, a few things pop out.

First, this story comes from a preindustrial age when the sun and seasons controlled the rhythm of life. Aesop lived in an era of subsistence farming, and all the wealth created that year was grown, stored, and eaten before it went bad.

Second, notice that a single grasshopper is speaking to a family of ants.

This raises questions in this postindustrial world ruled by the clock.

If the grasshopper spent his Time saving for the winter, would he ever be able to generate enough grain (wealth) on his own to find Time to play his fiddle? What was it about a family of ants, collectively spending Time, that allowed them to have enough grain (wealth) during the summer months, store some for the winter months, and also grow their family?

Why didn't Aesop talk about the farmer who grew the wheat?

What is it we are saving, and what are we saving it for?

We will answer these questions as we move through the next chapters.

What is important is that most people look at the clock or calendar, notice the passing of Time, and comment on how fast or slow it seems to move.

To hack the Time-Wealth Matrix, though, we need to understand that Time is our partner. Understanding how we perceive, use, and accumulate Time will be critical in hacking the Time-Wealth Matrix.

We will return to Time, but we must truly understand what money and wealth genuinely are to know how to work the calendar and clock to become wealthy.

"And in the end, it's not the years in your life that count. It's the life in your years."

—ABRAHAM LINCOLN

TAKEAWAYS

Time, our most precious resource, often goes unnoticed and undervalued when it appears abundant. Yet, like water in a drought or air in a scuba tank, its true worth is realized when it becomes scarce or fleeting.

Establishing systems that harness Time as our partner within our daily routines is crucial.

We all understand that Time is a depleting asset, but fortunately, we can store Time in the form of money and other assets, giving us flexibility in how we spend our Time if we don't want to work in the winter to earn our keep, like the ants in Aesop's fable.

Next, we must understand how money is created and how Time is stored.

CHAPTER 3

MONEY ISN'T WHAT YOU THINK IT IS

DEFINING MONEY

As an undergraduate, I took a course in money and banking in which the professor taught us the intricacies of money. We learned there were different types of money defined as M1 and M2, along with other classifications that economists use. We also learned how banks fit into the modern money system. Of course, as a young graduate, I thought I completely understood money.

Nope.

It has taken me many years in finance to truly understand what money is in today's fiat-currency world and how it fits into the Wealth Equation. What is fiat currency?

Well, by definition, the word "fiat" is an authoritative or arbitrary order.

This means fiat currency is considered money simply because a government has ordered us to treat it as money. Think about it; we exchange rectangular pieces of colored paper for food, video game consoles, and other necessities of life.

In countries like the US, where the currency is somewhat stable, it is safe to use. But in countries where the currency is unstable or scarce, people use alternatives to the country's currency. In some parts of Africa, cell phone minutes are used to buy food and other necessities.

Regardless of whether the currency is stable or unstable, it is only considered money because someone else said it is money, and we agreed to use it as such. It is paper pretending to be money. In reality, it is fake money.

Since we don't have an entire semester together, I've written my own fable on money to describe this better. As a fable, it leaves a lot out, so other professionals might quibble with the intricacies, but I hope you take away the lessons it is trying to impart.

THE FARMER GROWS VALUE
THE VALLEY

Once upon a time, there was a fertile valley surrounded by mountains.

THE FARMER

One day, a farmer stumbled on the valley and could see it was a great place to plant the kernels of wheat he was carrying. When the crop was ready, he reaped it, made bread, and fed his family. He was happy with the value he had created in the form of wheat.

THE FARMER MEETS THE BAKER—
THEY INVENT MONEY

One day, while the farmer was threshing the wheat so he could grind flour, a baker happened by. "For some of your wheat," he said, "I will make you all the bread you need for the year." The farmer, knowing the baker was better at baking, agreed to trade a pound of wheat for a pound of bread.

With this agreed-on exchange of value, they invented money.

Life continued, and this partnership worked quite well with the farmer farming and the baker baking.

THE FARMER AND THE BAKER MEET THE
BLACKSMITH—MONEY HITS A ROADBLOCK

During a bread-wheat exchange one day, a man approached the baker and said, "I see your gear is old. I'm a blacksmith and can make you a new oven in exchange for bread."

The baker loved this idea—a new oven would allow him to make more bread in a day, and they quickly agreed to exchange a pound of bread for a pound of ironworks.

The farmer, knowing his gear was old too, said, "I'll give you a pound of wheat in exchange for a pound of ironworks."

The blacksmith thought about it and said, "I don't need wheat, just bread. Is there anything else you offer?"

This is when the farmer realizes that only some appreciate and are willing to trade for the value created by farming.

THE FARMER, THE BAKER, THE BLACKSMITH, AND THE BANKER—THEY INVENT CURRENCY
THE BANKER ARRIVES

A well-dressed figure was listening as the farmer, the baker, and the blacksmith were trying to figure out how to work together.

Holding a heavy sack, he stepped forward and said, "I have the solution. I am a banker, and I want to start a bank in the valley. To get the bank started, I will split the one hundred one-pound coins I have in this sack. I will give the farmer twenty-five to buy a new plow, twenty-five to the baker to buy wheat, and twenty-five to the blacksmith to buy bread, and I will keep twenty-five coins to pay my way to live in such a beautiful valley and run my bank, which you all will use to keep your coins safe."

They all agreed that each one-pound coin would be equal to a pound of wheat, a pound of bread, or a pound of ironworks, and they called the coin the denarius, which was the name of the banker. This arrangement seemed reasonable to all, so they all shook hands in agreement.

Seems a bit crazy, but remember that over time people have used things such as cowrie shells, salt, tea bricks, and rai stones as currency to make trade easier.

This solved the farmer's problem since the blacksmith would accept this currency for new equipment.

THE FARMER, THE BAKER, THE BLACKSMITH, AND THE BANKER—THEY INVENT INFLATION

All went well until one day the banker took a vacation.

To fund his holiday, he sneakily scraped a bit off each coin. The banker believed his actions would go unnoticed, and he systematically repeated this scheme every year, methodically scraping off more of the coins to pay for his vacations.

Everything went flawlessly until the blacksmith realized the payment he received for his ironwork seemed light.

To ensure he wasn't being shortchanged, the blacksmith brought his coins and a pound of ironworks to the baker and the farmer to compare their weights. It turned out the pound of ironworks was heavier than one coin, and so was a pound of bread and a pound of wheat.

"You know what this means?" asked the farmer.

The baker and the blacksmith looked at him with curiosity, and the farmer answered, "A pound of wheat now costs two denarii."

The next day, when the banker came to buy bread, the baker told him, "A loaf of bread is now two denarii." The blacksmith told him, "The cost of iron is now two denarii per pound."

The banker realized the twenty-five coins he held could buy only half as much as they could the day before. He looked in the mirror and asked, "What have I done?"

Great question!

Let's break from this story and explain what has happened so far.

MONEY—WHAT IS IT?
PRODUCING VALUE

The farmer did not need the denarius. The value he created was from his farming skills, along with the Time he spent in the field raising wheat and turning it into bread. This means that Farming Skill × Time = Value.

$$\text{Skill} \times \text{Time} = \text{Value, or } S \times T = V$$

BARTER—EXCHANGING VALUE FOR
VALUE, ALSO CALLED MONEY

Once the baker arrived, he needed wheat to make bread. This is when the farmer and the baker agreed to exchange bread for wheat. This is what happened:

$$\text{Farmer: Skill} \times \text{Time} = \text{Value} = \text{Wheat} = \text{Money}$$

$$\text{Baker: Skill} \times \text{Time} = \text{Value} = \text{Bread} = \text{Money}$$

The skill and Time the farmer applied became wheat, which then became the money the farmer could trade for the baker's money, represented by the bread created by his skill and Time.

This is the earliest form of money. This exchange system is called barter.

IMPORTANT: The word "money" in this example is simply representing the value created by the farmer and the baker's skill and Time. Without skill and Time, money does not exist because bread and wheat then do not exist. After all, the value was never created.

This system worked great until the blacksmith showed up.

ENTER THE BANKER—THE CENTRAL
BANK AND GOVERNMENT THAT IS

This is the problem with barter. As the world grows in population, finding others who need precisely the value/money created by each person's skill and Time becomes harder and harder.

Example: How much wheat should be exchanged for a pair of socks?

The farmer could not trade with the blacksmith because there was nothing the blacksmith needed from the farmer. Yet the farmer needed tools from the blacksmith.

This is when the banker showed up.

The banker's contribution to the valley was currency, not money.

This needs a brief explanation; the farmer, baker, and blacksmith are actual producers of value. The banker in my story, though thinly disguised, is the government, and it is not a value producer. The government printing presses and policies create money for trade, which is helpful. The printing presses and policies also help create inflation, which is not helpful.

The banker did not spend any Time or skill in making the coins. The denarius gained value simply because all the citizens agreed it represented something of value. I will expand on this later in the book, but for now, know that inflation is like the banker scraping the coins.

In the farmer's case, Skill × Time = Wheat = 1 lb of Wheat = Money = 1 denarius

Currency allowed the farmer to trade with the blacksmith even though he had nothing the blacksmith needed. The denarius represented the value the blacksmith could take to buy bread from the baker.

But what if people did not agree on the value of your currency?

Imagine being on the street in Paris in 1777, and you have ten loaves of bread and ten Continental notes, the currency issued by the American Continental Congress at the time. No Frenchman would want your Continentals, but you could sell the bread for French currency and buy your ticket on a French ship headed to America, where everyone agrees on what a Continental (our denarius) was worth.

Currency is valuable because the people using it agree it is valuable.

ROCK'S MUSINGS

The value you create is money. The currency (dollar bills) you get represents the value you create. Don't confuse your value with currency. Your value is real. The currency is pretending to be value, but it is fake.

Remember, money existed before the banker showed up with the denarius. The problem was that before the denarius showed up, money was messy! Currency makes trade easier because it is fungible. Fungible means every coin has exactly the same value as any other coin (so no calculating how much wheat to exchange for socks), and all agree on its value.

CURRENCY—WHAT IS IT GOOD FOR?

In our postindustrial world, currency has no intrinsic value.

To put this in context, if a person were lost in the woods for a couple of days, would they rather have a hundred-dollar bill or a couple loaves of bread?

Today's money is simply slips of paper or digital notes on a bank's balance sheet. We all just agree that a dollar is a dollar.

While currencies have no intrinsic value, they are helpful in our day-to-day lives. Currency has two purposes: active and passive.

ACTIVE CURRENCY—SPENDING

We can spend money for one of two reasons: current consumption or Time savings.

Current consumption is if the currency just received is spent to cover immediate expenses: rent, food, movies, video games, or bungee jumping. This currency is the value transferred to someone else for the value they create.

> We work forty hours a week. The paycheck the company just deposited into the bank is *currency just received* and represents the value we created over the previous forty hours.

The blacksmith will exchange a denarius for bread because he needs to eat.

The exchange of currency for something that allows the production of more value in the same amount of Time leads to time savings. The baker will trade the denarius with the blacksmith because the new oven would let him bake more bread in the same Time.

The blacksmith's exchange was for current consumption, and the baker's exchange was for Time savings.

PASSIVE CURRENCY—ACCUMULATION

The baker could bake more bread in the same Time with the new oven. When he exchanged his value (bread) for denarius (currency), he received more than he needed for current consumption.

The baker gave this excess denarius to the banker to hold for the future.

Specialization and the Accumulation of Value

An enormous benefit of currency and trade is that it allows the farmer, baker, and blacksmith to specialize. Since they spared the farmer the need to turn the wheat into flour and then bread, he had Time to plant more wheat, which he could save in case there was a bad harvest. The baker could make more bread because he did not have to grow the wheat. The blacksmith did more ironwork, since he did not need to grow his own food.

As the valley continued to flourish and more travelers passed through, they could trade this excess value (wheat, bread, and ironworks) for more currency than they needed for active spending, so they gave it to the banker to hold for them until they needed it. This saving with the banker allowed them to store the excess currency.

Remember,

$$\text{Currency} = \text{Value} = \text{Skill} \times \text{Time}$$

The excess currency (denarius) allowed the farmer, the baker, and the blacksmith to store/bank the extra currency and spend it later. The significant advantage of currency is that it will not spoil in the granary like wheat, mold on the shelf like bread, or become an obsolete tool like ironwork.

Savings—What We Really Save Is Time

This next part is tricky but crucial.

The farmer plants the seed in the spring, tends the crop over the summer, harvests it in the fall, and then takes it to market to exchange for denarius (currency). He then deposits the denarius in the bank, goes home, and waits for the next season to do it again.

When the farmer walks into the bank, he carries the skill and Time harvested from the last season.

$$\text{Skill} \times \text{Time} = \text{Value} = \text{Money} = \text{Denarius}$$

Here is the tricky part: after he deposits the denarius and walks out of the bank, he carries his skill with him. After all, he knows how to grow crops for the next season taking nothing out of the bank.

The part of the equation (Skill × Time) left behind at the bank is Time.

People can save excess Time as passive currency to use in the future.

$$\text{Passive Currency} = \text{Time} = \text{Money}$$

All the farmer, the baker, and the blacksmith need to do is put this with the banker, and, later on, they can take it out and buy what they need without spending Time growing wheat, baking bread, or making iron tools all over again. The Time is stored; it is safe.

Unless…

"Pennies do not come from heaven. They have to be earned here on earth."

—Margaret Thatcher

THE YIN AND YANG OF CURRENCY
CURRENCY'S NEMESIS—INFLATION

When the banker shaved a little off each coin, he devalued the stored Time associated with each coin. The banker changed the Value Equation to

$$\text{Denarius} = \text{Time} \div 2$$

Yesterday, one denarius could buy what now takes two denarii. While the townsfolk had the skills to replace what was lost, they couldn't turn back time to farm the last season.

The banker stole the Time they had stored.

When the farmer, the baker, and the blacksmith recalculated what their coins were worth, they could square the circle by doubling their prices. Going forward in the valley,

$$2 \text{ denarii} = 1 \text{ pound of wheat} = 1 \text{ pound}$$
$$\text{of bread} = 1 \text{ pound of steel}$$

Easy enough in a make-believe valley. Unfortunately, we must leave the valley, which is where things get more difficult.

Currency Debasement and Inflation

What the banker did is known as currency debasement: reducing the actual value of a coin but pretending it is the same value. The result is inflation.

A brief history lesson is needed here: there was a real denarius coin during Roman times, and its deliberate debasement led to inflation, which, along with other issues, led to the collapse of the Roman Empire.[21]

The denarius coin was introduced in 211 BC, containing

nearly 95 percent silver, and it facilitated trade across the empire. The stability of the coin encouraged commerce and contributed to Rome's prosperity. The debasement of the denarius occurred over several centuries:

- Early Debasement (first century AD)—Under emperors like Augustus and Nero, the silver content was reduced to around 80 percent.
- Continued Debasement (second century AD)—During the reigns of emperors like Marcus Aurelius and Commodus, the silver content dropped to about 75 percent.
- Rapid Debasement (third century AD)—The reigns of emperors such as Septimius and Severus in the third century saw a dramatic acceleration in debasement. By the mid-century, the silver content had plummeted to around 50 percent; by the time of Gallienus, it was as low as 5 percent.

The consequences of this sustained debasement were profound. As the purity of the denarius declined, its value dropped sharply. Hyperinflation set in, and trust in the currency eroded. The once intricate economic system that had supported the empire unraveled.

The Roman population, like the inhabitants of the valley, endured debasement. Every day, citizens faced skyrocketing prices for necessities, while savings stored in denarii rapidly lost value. The erosion of trust in the currency led to a slowing of economic growth, affecting employment and quality of life across all social classes.

After lasting almost a thousand years, the fall of Rome signaled the end of Imperial Rome in 476 AD.[22]

Historically, kings, emperors, and governments have used actual silver and gold in the coins they minted. While made of paper, United States dollars were once convertible into gold or silver.

Not anymore.

In 1971, the US government decreed that gold no longer backed the dollar. By government fiat, we were told that a dollar was worth a dollar because the government promised to protect its value. Like the coins in the valley, this fiat currency has no intrinsic value except for what everyone agrees it is worth.

And, like the banker in the fable, the government has done a lousy job of protecting the dollar. Since 1971, according to the US Department of Labor inflation calculator, the value of $1.00 fell to $0.14 by the end of 2022.[23]

Value of $1 over Time

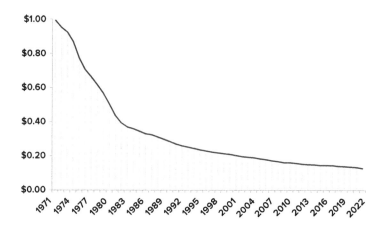

You will need about:

- $7.48 to buy what $1.00 bought in 1971.
- $3.83 to buy what $1.00 bought in 1980.
- $1.29 to buy what $1.00 bought in 2013.

THE BAD NEWS

Let's put this in terms of Time.

Let's assume the farmer needed a dollar a day in 1980 to be comfortable in retirement, or $365.00 a year. In 1980, the farmer put $365.00 in the bank to pay for his first year of retirement: January 1 to December 31, 2023.

Because of inflation, when he collects the currency in 2023, that money will pay only for the things he needs until April.

The banker and inflation have stolen about nine months of Time from the farmer.

If money loses value, it is fake money.

THE GOOD NEWS

The good news is if currency has a nemesis, it must also have a hero. This hero must have the superpower of keeping up with or outpacing inflation over the long term.

CURRENCY'S HERO—COMPOUNDING INTEREST

It's time for a tale about a different farmer. Instead of wheat, this farmer grows water lilies and sells them in garden stores.

THE WATER LILY PAYS INTEREST

Imagine a farmer who began his venture with just a single water lily and a pond. Every night, the water lily multiplies, producing one new plant. The farmer collects this fresh lily every morning and sells it to the local garden center.

It's a decent business that brings in enough income for him to cover his daily expenses.

THE FARMER HELPS A FRIEND

One day, the farmer receives an urgent call from a friend living in a different town. His friend is sick, and his farm needs tending while he recovers. Without a second thought, the farmer packs up and leaves to help.

His friend's recovery took longer than expected; it was exactly 511 days.

Upon his return home late in the afternoon, the farmer checks on his pond, hoping his water lilies have survived. To his surprise, water lilies cover his pond, and there is space for just one more.

The following morning, he discovers the original water lily has produced one more, and it now entirely covers the pond.

From this, the farmer learns an important lesson: it takes exactly 512 days for the water lilies to cover his pond completely.

THE FARMER BUYS ANOTHER POND
AND A NEW TYPE OF WATER LILY

The farmer makes quite a profit by selling all his water lilies to multiple garden stores. With this newfound wealth, he makes two significant investments. First, he purchases the pond next to his, expanding his operation. Second, he buys a new strain of water lily.

Unlike his original water lilies, where only the original plant could sprout a new plant daily, this new strain offers something different. The parent lily can produce a fresh lily each day, and each of these offspring lilies can also sprout a new lily daily.

The next morning, the farmer heads to his ponds and counts four water lilies. Two in his original pond and two in his recently purchased pond. He lets the plants multiply for a few days before harvesting them.

The next day, as expected, he finds three lilies in the original pond, but, as the label on his new lilies showed, he finds four in the new pond.

Intrigued, he let the plants continue to grow. Over the following days, the lilies in the original pond steadily increase by one per day. After nine days, he has nine new water lilies.

The new pond continues to amaze him, with the number of lilies doubling each day: 4, then 8, then 16, 32, 64, 128, and 256.

After just nine days, the new pond is half full of water lilies, while the old pond has only nine. On the tenth day, the farmer is astounded to find the original pond only has ten lilies, while the new pond is completely covered. What took the original pond 512 days to accomplish, the new pond achieved in just ten days with the new strain of water lilies.

These ponds illustrate the difference between simple and compound interest. Simple interest is like the growth in the first pond, earning a steady, predictable increase on the original amount. In contrast, compound interest, represented by the explosive growth in the new pond, is the process of earning interest not only on the initial amount but also on the interest gained before.

WHEN THE BANKER PAYS TO HOLD YOUR MONEY

In the valley, the original banker only offered to hold Time (denarius) for the others.

A new banker moved to the valley and offered the citizens a simple interest program. He said, "Put one hundred denarii with me, and my bank will pay you 7.2 percent simple interest each year, and in ten years, you will get back 172 denarii."

The original banker, realizing he needs to outdo his new competitor, offers the same 7.2 percent, but on a compounding basis. He says to the citizens of the valley, "Put one hundred denarii with me, and in ten years, you will get back two hundred denarii."

THE RULE OF 72

Back in the real world, we use dollars to represent stored Time. Based on the preceding example, it only makes sense to compound Time stored with the banker, and there is a complicated math formula we can learn for the exact computation of compound interest. Instead of a math lesson, here is a hack that provides a close approximation:

$$72 \div \text{Interest Rate} = \text{Years to Double}$$

This means money doubles in about ten years at 7.2 percent or in 7.2 years at 10 percent.

And since this is math, it works every time!

The following chart lets you know when your money will double at different rates:

This is the Rule of 72.

Rule of 72

Easy Hack to Estimate When Money Doubles

% Rate	Approximate Number of Years to Double
1	72
2	36
3	24
4	18
5	14
6	12
7	10
8	9
9	8
10	7
11	7
12	6

And what the water lily farmer—and investors throughout history—have learned is that the most important doubling of value is the last one. That is the one that takes your pond from being half covered to being completely covered.

"Money and inflation compound. Make sure your money compounds faster than your government's inflation."

—Rock

TAKEAWAYS

Skills and Time come together to create value. If we lived on the frontier, miles from others, we would survive on the value we created: food, housing, fire, etc. We would not need money.

Once a year, when we would travel to our neighbor's house, we would load the wagon with value we produced, like eggs. With our eggs, we would barter for things we need but cannot produce, like salt. Our eggs exchanged for our neighbor's salt would be an exchange of value. Our eggs become money, which is another word for value.

When a town popped up, we made our once-a-year trip into town instead of to our neighbor. We exchanged our eggs with the baker, but we did not want his cakes, so he gave us currency instead. With this currency, we could go to the grocer, miller, or doctor. The currency pretends to be the value of our eggs. Remember, currency is only valuable because we all agree it is valuable.

Sadly, since currency is just pretending, inflation can steadily erode it. To preserve the value of our accumulated wealth, we need to compound currency faster than inflation can diminish it. This is where understanding the Rule of 72 and how Time is our partner impacts our wealth.

We need to learn to invest our funds and allow them to grow over Time.

CHAPTER 4

INVESTING ISN'T WHAT YOU THINK IT IS

DEFINING INVESTING

In our modern, clock-driven world, financial markets have become incredibly complex. Many individuals devote their entire lives to deciphering these markets, using terms like Alpha, Beta, Delta, Vega, and Rho to describe them.

For regular folks, though, investing typically boils down to two important steps:

- Accumulating passive currency
- Entrusting passive currency to someone else, known as a counterparty

Our bank accounts, 401(k) accounts, and IRAs are typical places to accumulate currency. Once we have accumulated currency, it is the time to hand it off to someone to invest for us—the counterparty.

Now is the time to do due diligence on the counterparty and the investment itself:

- Who are they (length of time in business, experience)?
- What do they intend to do with your currency?
- How do they profit from it?
- When can you expect your currency to be returned, along with any earnings?

The risk of investing is that this counterparty might return significantly less than it had initially projected from the investment.

For instance, consider a scenario in which you lend $100 to your cousin, who is now the counterparty.

The risks involved here include getting paid back in full, receiving less than what you lent, or, worst-case scenario, the counterparty (your deadbeat cousin) not returning any of your currency. This is a permanent loss of currency/Time.

INVESTING IS A COMMITMENT OF TIME TO EARN A RETURN

To help describe this in more detail, let's return to the valley.

THE FARMER, THE BAKER, AND THE BLACKSMITH USE ACTIVE TIME TO PAY CURRENT BILLS

Every morning, the residents of the valley wake up and go to work. It is this work (Skill × Time) that allows them to generate money that allows them to live in the valley.

Every day they make investment decisions:

- Harvest this field or plow that field?
- Bake loaves of bread or bake birthday cakes?
- Make a plow for the farmer or make an oven for the baker?

They have limited Time each day, so each investment decision comes with a cost. Each decision entails a trade-off because choosing one thing means losing the potential benefits of another. Economists call this opportunity cost.

Consider the decision between taking the fastest route versus the scenic route on vacation. Both options have advantages and disadvantages, but we must make a choice at the beginning of the journey. Taking the fastest route gets us to our beach chair sooner but comes with the stress of superhighways and lots of other vacationers heading in the same direction. The scenic route, while delaying the beach, offers a more relaxed travel experience and the possibility of stumbling upon some fantastic roadside attractions.

This is opportunity cost.

Another example of opportunity cost is taking a day off.

Those who work an eight-hour shift accumulate two hours in the form of PTO (paid time off). Those who decide to stay home consume eight hours of their PTO.

Both groups receive the same paycheck, but the folks who went to work accumulate an additional two hours of PTO for future use. In comparison, the second group spends eight hours of PTO and forfeits the opportunity to accrue two more hours of PTO. Therefore, choosing to stay home means sacrificing ten hours of potential earnings.

The opportunity cost of working might be missing a child's class play or postponing a round of golf with close friends.

Every day, everyone wakes up and decides how to use their Time. They make two decisions: one concerning active Time and another concerning accumulated Time.

The first decision is whether to work today and earn more accumulated Time or to spend accumulated Time. A young parent might choose to work to accumulate more Time, whereas a retired individual might opt to spend their accumulated Time.

The second decision is where to put accumulated Time (currency) to compound.

The farmer can keep it in his sock drawer, which breaks down like this:

- Who is the counterparty? The sock drawer.
- What does the sock drawer do with the passive currency? Nothing.
- When will it be returned? Whenever the drawer is opened.

Farmer

Account	Owned	Owed
Sock Drawer	$1,000	$0
Savings Account	$0	$0
Loans	$0	$0
Total	$1,000	$0
Net Worth		**$1,000**

Keeping track of our money means knowing where it is located, what we own, and to whom we owe money that needs to be repaid. Subtracting what we owe other people from what we own is what accountants call our net worth. On paper, it looks like this:

Keeping the passive currency in the sock drawer is safe, but it does not compound.

The farmer's worth is $1,000.

What are the other options?

THE BANKER STORES THE TOWNSFOLKS' PASSIVE TIME FOR THE FUTURE

We are told the bank is a safe place to store money. Put passive currency into a savings account, and we can draw it out when needed and earn interest while it sits there.

What if the farmer uses the bank instead of the sock drawer? Let's explore this a bit.

- Who is the farmer's counterparty? The bank.
- What does the banker do with the passive currency? Lend it to others for cars, homes, and businesses.
- When will it be returned to the farmer? One year from today, with interest.

So far, so good.

Let's track this transaction: the farmer takes $1,000 out of his sock drawer and gives it to the banker, who promises to give back the $1,000 plus $30, 365 days from now. This is 3 percent interest.

Farmer				Banker		
Account	**Owned**	**Owed**		**Account**	**Owned**	**Owed**
Sock Drawer	$0	$0		Sock Drawer	$0	$0
Savings Account	$1,000	$0		Savings Account	$1,000	$1,000
Loans	$0	$0		Loans	$0	$0
Total	$1,000	$0		Total	$1,000	$1,000
Net Worth		$1,000		Net Worth		$0

The farmer lent his passive currency to the banker. The farmer now owns a loan called a savings account. The banker has the farmer's cash in the bank's vault, but the banker also owes the farmer $1,000 plus 3 percent at the end of the twelve months.

However, no additional creations have been made at this time.

The farmer still owns $1,000, but the banker's worth is zero because, while he now owns $1,000 in cash, he also owes $1,000 to the farmer—Own*ed* minus Owed.

The significance of the letter *N* is highlighted in the stark difference between the words "owned" and "owed." This single letter shifts the entire meaning—the difference between possessing something and being in debt is crucial in determining one's financial standing.

Compounding Time

What does the banker do with the farmer's passive currency?

The banker lends it out to the baker and the blacksmith, so they can buy supplies. The banker lends $500 to the baker and

$500 to the blacksmith. He also has them sign a piece of paper that says in 365 days, they will pay back $525. This is a loan at 5 percent interest.

- Who is the banker's counterparty? The baker and the blacksmith.
- What do they do with the passive currency? Buy supplies for their businesses, making it active currency.
- When will the borrower return it to the banker? One year from today, with interest.

Day 1

On day one, the farmer lends his money to the banker at 3 percent, and the banker lends this money to the baker and the blacksmith at 5 percent. The baker buys flour, and the blacksmith buys iron, knowing they can double this money in one year's time.

The farmer's worth is $1,000, while the banker's worth is $0 (the banker lends the same amount he owes), and the baker and the blacksmith's worths are $0 each since they bought supplies equal to what they borrowed. When we add up everyone's worth (owned minus owed), we can see, despite a lot of activity, that nothing has been created yet.

Farmer

Account	Owned	Owed
Sock Drawer	$0	$0
Savings Account	$1,000	$0
Loans	$0	$0
Total	$1,000	$0
Net Worth		$1,000

Banker

Account	Owned	Owed
Sock Drawer	$0	$0
Savings Account	$0	$1,000
Loans	$1,000	$0
Total	$1,000	$1,000
Net Worth		$0

Baker

Account	Owned	Owed
Sock Drawer	$0	$0
Savings Account	$0	$0
Supplies	$500	$0
Loans	$0	$500
Total	$500	$500
Net Worth		$0

Blacksmith

Account	Owned	Owed
Sock Drawer	$0	$0
Savings Account	$0	$0
Supplies	$500	$0
Loans	$0	$500
Total	$500	$500
Net Worth		$0

The only person with net worth on day one is the farmer with his $1,000 put into the savings accounts.

Day 365

One year later, the baker sells the bread he baked for $1,000, and the blacksmith sells the tools he manufactured for $1,000, and then all the money is reversed.

This is when the magic happens!

The baker and the blacksmith pay the banker. The banker puts $30 into the farmer's saving account, and $20 into his own savings account. The baker and blacksmith put the money they earned into their own savings accounts, that look like this:

Farmer

Account	Owned	Owed
Sock Drawer	$0	$0
Savings Account	$1,030	$0
Loans	$0	$0
Total	$1,030	$0
Net Worth		$1,030

Banker

Account	Owned	Owed
Sock Drawer	$0	$0
Savings Account	$20	$0
Loans	$0	$0
Total	$20	$0
Net Worth		$20

Baker

Account	Owned	Owed
Sock Drawer	$0	$0
Savings Account	$475	$0
Supplies	$0	$0
Loans	$0	$0
Total	$475	$0
Net Worth		$475

Blacksmith

Account	Owned	Owed
Sock Drawer	$0	$0
Savings Account	$475	$0
Supplies	$0	$0
Loans	$0	$0
Total	$475	$0
Net Worth		$475

On Day 1, there was a starting balance of $1,000, but by Day 365, it had doubled to $2,000. There is $30 for the farmer (3 percent) and $20 for the banker (2 percent), and the baker and the blacksmith each netted $475 for their work for $950.

It is clear that Time × Skill netted $475 for the baker and the blacksmith, totaling $950.

But why did the farmer and the banker make money?

Interest.

But what is interest?

Other people's Time.

Huh?

Let's assume the baker and the blacksmith work eight hours every day for one year (2,920 hours) for a combined 5,840 hours. Each made $2.74 per eight-hour day or $1,000 for the year. On Day 365, the baker pays back the banker the $525 and keeps $475. The blacksmith does the same.

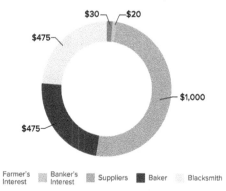

How Is the $2,000 Earned by the Baker and Blacksmith Split?

$30 · $20 · $475 · $1,000 · $475

Farmer's Interest · Banker's Interest · Suppliers · Baker · Blacksmith

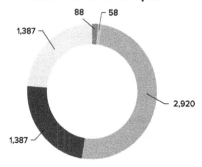

How Are the Hours the Baker and Blacksmith Worked Split?

88 · 58 · 1,387 · 2,920 · 1,387

Remember, they borrowed the money to purchase flour and iron. They would not need to borrow the money to purchase these items if they had the money saved. They would have each earned $500 after their costs, not $475. The allocation of Time and money over the 365 days looks like this:

Time Allocation Chart — Day 365

Time Is Divided between	Baker		Blacksmith		Total	
	Dollars	Hours	Dollars	Hours	Dollars	Hours
Farmer's Interest	$15	44	$15	44	$30	88
Banker's Interest	$10	29	$10	29	$20	58
Total Interest Paid	$25	73	$25	73	$50	146
Suppliers	$500	1,460	$500	1460	$1,000	2,920
Profit	$475	1,387	$475	1,387	$950	2,774
Total	$1,000	2,920	$1,000	2,920	$2,000	5,840

The farmer and the banker received $50, which equals 146 hours of other people's Time, and they split it into $30 and $20. In Time, the farmer received eighty-eight hours and the banker fifty-eight hours.

The farmer lent his passive currency (stored Time) to allow the others to make money. The farmer's passive currency becomes an active currency that the others use to pay their bills.

We should talk about the banker in this equation.

The farmer saved the money he earned because of the work

he had done in the fields. What did the banker do to receive his fifty-eight hours of other people's Time?

The banker took on a risk. In this situation, the banker promised the farmer a safe 3 percent return. The farmer's risk is with the banker.

When the banker lent the funds to the baker and the blacksmith, there was a risk they would not pay the funds back. In this situation, it breaks down like this:

- Who is the banker's counterparty? The baker and the blacksmith.
- What do they do with the farmer's passive currency? Buy flour and iron.
- When will the banker receive the return? In one year, including interest.

If all goes well, the baker and the blacksmith pay up.

But what happens if the baker or the blacksmith do not pay back the funds?

The banker still owes the farmer a return. This is the banker's risk. The banker's skill is knowing who will and will not repay the funds.

Moreover, things happen even if the blacksmith and the baker are good risks on their own. The bakery could burn down, and the blacksmith might be injured—the list of possibilities goes on and on. While these are low-probability events, they happen.

But the bakery and the foundry are highly unlikely to burn down simultaneously. Lending to two people reduces the risk. The banker could reduce the risk further by spreading the currency between the baker, the blacksmith, the mill owner, and the saloon owner. It is unlikely that all these businesses would burn down simultaneously.

Spreading this risk across various entities in different places, run by different people, and doing different things is called diversification. Or, as our mothers taught us, don't put all your eggs in one basket!

The farmer can reduce the counterparty risk of the banker by putting the passive currency in two banks instead of one.

Wow, that's a lot of activity just to open a savings account!

"Those who understand interest earn it, while those who don't pay it."
—ALBERT EINSTEIN

SKIP THE BANKER AND USE THE ACCUMULATED TIME DIRECTLY

The next investing question becomes whether an investor should take on more risk than just giving money to the banker. The answer is probably yes!

The Farmer Lends the Baker Time—This Is a Loan

Lending directly to the baker (the counterparty) removes the banker and allows the farmer (lender) to earn all the interest (other people's Time) that goes along with the agreement.

Here is a situation in which the baker and the farmer are friends and decide to bypass the banker. The baker agrees to borrow $1,000 at 4 percent from the farmer.

This is more than the banker pays for passive currency deposits but less than the banker charges to lend currency.

One person or bank lending to another person or business is known as a loan.

Here is the biggest risk: the baker's business fails and cannot return the money to the farmer.

This is known as event risk.

The Farmer and the Blacksmith Lend the
Farmer Time—This Is a Bond

To diversify the event risk, the farmer and the blacksmith team up ($500 each) to lend the baker $1,000 at 4 percent.

Now if the baker cannot pay back the funds, they each lose $500 instead of the farmer losing $1000.

To diversify the event risk further, the farmer could have the blacksmith, mill owner, and saloon owner all join him in lending to the baker. Many people pooling their funds to lend is called a bond.

The Farmer, the Baker, and the Blacksmith Pool
Their Time and Build a Mill—This Is a Stock

While talking about how well business is going, a person approaches the farmer, the baker, and the blacksmith at the bar. This person, an experienced miller, proposes pooling their passive currency and giving it to him to build a gristmill. The mill will grind wheat for the valley more effectively than anyone has done in the past. This is a risky proposition, and the new person does not want to borrow the money, but if the farmer, the baker, and the blacksmith invest in his business, he will share all the profits with them.

After much discussion, they all agree, the mill is built, and they each own 25 percent of the mill building, the land it sits on, and the profits it generates. The farmer, the baker, and the blacksmith contribute currency, and the miller contributes his skill.

- Who is the farmer, baker, and blacksmith's counterparty? The miller.
- What does the counterparty do with the currency? Build and operate a mill.
- When will the passive currency be returned? Never, but the owners will receive income from the mill for as long as it operates. A stock differs from a loan because the money invested is not expected to be returned from the company that it is invested in. It is a contribution of capital that turns passive currency into active currency. The return is the income generated from the business.

The mill owner hires employees to run the mill day to day. The employees come to work every day for the next 365 days and grind wheat. Every two weeks, the mill owner pays the employees for their hours of work (Milling Skill × Time).

Once a month, the mill owner does the math and puts 25 percent of the profits (his ownership percentage) into his bank account. The mill owner's work is knowing who to hire, managing, ensuring the product is good quality, and selling the product.

The other 75 percent of the profits (the others' ownership percentage) goes to another bank account. At the end of the year, they equally split the profits among the farmer, the baker, and the blacksmith.

After the initial passive-currency investment, the farmer, the baker, and the blacksmith never worked in the mill. Indeed, the mill was located a fair distance from the town, so they never saw it.

But once a year, the mill owner came to town and paid the profits to the other owners. But where did this profit come from?

It came from other people's Time. But which other people?

- The suppliers were paid for their wares and the Time needed to create them.
- The employees received the paychecks for their Time they agreed to when hired.

Who is left?
The customers.
Huh?
Well, each of the customers of the mill could have grown their own wheat, harvested it, and then ground it into flour. However, each customer of the mill independently determined that it was faster, easier, and less expensive for them to spend some of their Time as active currency to purchase flour than to make it on their own.

The return the owners receive for risking their capital in a business venture, which may or may not yield a profit, is called dividends. Unlike a loan, dividends are not a guaranteed repayment of capital. They represent the effective management skills of those in control who have efficiently managed costs, leading to profit.

The farmer, the baker, the blacksmith, and the miller own the mill's profits, building, land, and equipment. They share any fluctuation in the mill's value, whether it increases or decreases.

The Owners Sell Stock to the Barkeep in an IPO

The mill has been thriving for a few years now. During a routine profit-sharing meeting, the saloon owner approaches the four mill owners with a proposal to join their venture. As friends, they agree to each contribute 5 percent of their stake, selling 20 percent of the business to the saloon owner.

However, since the saloon owner's risk is considerably lower when buying into an already successful business rather than starting from scratch, the mill owners increase the price by 20 percent. This provides them with a profit on their initial investment, in addition to the income they have been receiving from the mill.

This transaction marks the first time the shares of the business are available to an outside investor; hence, it's referred to as an initial public offering (IPO). This IPO allows the original investors to convert a previously illiquid asset (the mill, the land, and the equipment) into currency, which they can put in the bank, reinvest in their businesses, or invest in other ventures.

The Farmer, the Baker, and the Blacksmith Exchange Stock with the Barkeep and the Banker—This Is a Stock Market

Indeed, the reinvestment begins. With the money generated in the IPO, each of the mill owners starts to slowly sell a portion of his business:

- The farmer gains a stake in the baker's business.
- The baker invests in the blacksmith's business.
- The saloon owner buys into the banker's business.

Then, an interesting development occurs: the farmer thinks the banker's business has more upside than the baker's. He sells his interest in the baker's business to the blacksmith, who wants to be part owner of one of his customers, locking in his business there. The farmer then purchases the saloon owner's stake in the banker's business. With this cash, the saloon owner opens another location that should make more profit than his investment in the bank.

These transactions constitute a stock market. A stock market is a venue where willing participants buy and sell shares in companies they've invested in. The investors buy or sell from each other based on their future expectations for the stock or their cash flow needs.

Importantly, these transactions occur among investors, not with the original company they're investing in. The company is indifferent to who the owners are; they pay the profits to whoever owns the shares.

DEFINING INVESTMENTS IN THE MODERN ERA

No matter how complicated it seems, a bond is just a big loan that a bunch of people pooling their passive currency lend to someone to make it active currency, and they earn interest on the amount owed.

A stock is just individuals owning the risk of a company's future earnings.

An IPO is just the owners of a company offering to let other people become owners and share the risk of the future.

A stock market is just all the owners of all the companies trading those shares with each other based on what they think the future holds for each company.

In today's postindustrial world, all this goes on every day, and billions of shares are traded daily across the world.[24] In 2022, global stock markets totaled $124 trillion and bond markets $126 trillion.[25]

WHAT MAKES A COMPANY VALUABLE?

In our world, where the clock drives economic activity, the value of an enterprise is the Time it saves or occupies for its users.

Let's consider the average person who works around 2,000 hours annually and makes about $55,000 or $27.50 per hour.[26] How are the hours or money spent?

Take our morning coffee, for instance: 66 percent of the US population are coffee drinkers, with 28 percent opting for coffee brewed outside their homes.[27]

Do we need coffee? No.

Do we want coffee? Yes!

According to CNET,[28] the cost to brew one twelve-ounce drip at home is $0.62 versus $1.85 at Starbucks. (Unless you live in New York City! Oh, and these are 2022 prices. Remember that inflation thing?)

Assuming that consumption is one cup per day, this results in the following:

- Thirty-four percent of people spend no Time on coffee.
- Thirty-eight percent of people spend one day a year working to pay for their love of coffee, or $226.
- Twenty-eight percent spend about $675 per year on coffee, which means they work about three days a year for their coffee.

To put this in context, Starbucks had net revenues of $32.3 billion dollars in the fiscal year 2022.[29]

Starbucks Corporation (NASDAQ: SBUX) today announced that its Board of Directors has approved a quarterly cash dividend of $0.53 per share of outstanding Common Stock. The dividend will be payable in cash on February 24, 2023 to shareholders of record on February 10, 2023.[30]

Starbucks scooped up a lot of other people's Time and gave it to the company's owners.

Next, what car do you drive to work? According to Kelly Blue Book:

- A 2022 Chevy Spark costs about $13,000 or 473 hours of the average worker's Time.
- A 2022 BMW 2 Series costs about $36,000 or 1,309 hours.

According to CNBC, in 2022, General Motors had an operating profit of $15 billion or $7.25 per share for its owners.[31] BMW rewarded its owners with about $9.00 per share in 2022.[32]

It goes on:

- Make your lunch at home or go to Red Robin?
- Make your clothes or go to Nordstrom or Walmart?

Every purchase we make moves a little of our Time to someone else. And these are things we need or want that can be touched.

What about things that can't be touched, like music?

Check this out: Don McLean and Gerry Rafferty reportedly earn $300,000 and $100,000 a year from "American Pie" and "Baker Street," respectively.[33]

"American Pie" occupies eight minutes of a listener's Time. Enough people give Don McLean eight minutes of their Time to total the equivalent of 5.5 years of average earnings every year. Listeners have played Ed Sheeran's "Shape of You" over one billion times on Spotify.[34] We pay for Spotify monthly, and

Don McLean and Ed Sheeran get paid a part of that every time someone takes their Time to listen to one of their songs.

HOW THE AVERAGE FAMILY SPENDS ITS TIME

How does the average household spend the Time that is earned?[35]

Spending by Category

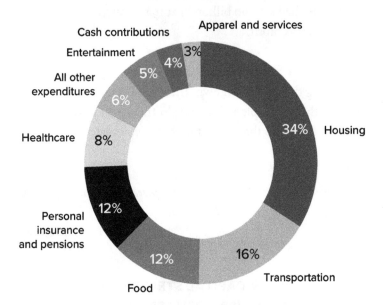

In today's world, driven by the clock rather than the sun and the seasons, we no longer live as self-sufficient pioneers who build log cabins and farm the land. Instead, most of us work for a company that pays for our Time and skills, along with those of all of our coworkers. They take this work and mold it into something more valuable, which they then sell to others.

The profit is taken after they pay for the total cost of production, including the employees' work. The profit represents other people's Time.

Some of the biggest companies that collect other people's Time are:[36]

- Walmart—earned $514.40 billion in revenue in 2019, of which $6.67 billion was profit.
- Exxon Mobil—had $290.21 billion in 2019 revenue, of which $20.84 billion was profit.
- Apple—had $265.60 billion in 2019 revenue, of which $59.53 billion was profit.

People buy from these companies because it is more efficient than doing things on their own. The result is that the companies that do things people want, and do them really well, collect more of the Time the population has accumulated.

"When you buy a bond, you're betting on the solvency of the issuer. When you buy a stock, you're buying a piece of a living organism with a potentially unlimited lifespan."

—Charlie Munger

YOUR CAPITAL STRUCTURE: BORROWER, SPENDER, LENDER, OWNER, AND COUNTING TIME

In finance, we focus on capital markets and capital structure.

Capital markets are like the toolbox for finance—they include different ways to save and invest money, like the savings accounts, bonds, and stocks we just reviewed.

A person's capital structure is simpler; it's all about where the value we accumulate goes. What is spent, what is owed, and what is owned. Understanding the different components of this structure and learning to balance them is essential for everyone, especially when managing their own money.

WHAT IS A BORROWER?

A borrower takes Time from the future to use in the present.

Huh?

An example might help here: Suppose a person named Matrix decides to go on a $2,000 cruise vacation with friends. Matrix has no savings, so he charges the trip to a credit card. After a fantastic journey, Matrix returns, happy, tanned, and relaxed.

The following month, the credit card bill arrives, and Matrix can only afford to pay off $100 for the cruise. At this rate, because of interest on the credit card, it takes thirty-six months or $3,600 to pay off the $2,000 cruise.

Matrix has fully committed $3,600 of future earnings to the bank.

Let's assume that Matrix's hourly rate is $25.00. For the next thirty-six months, Matrix dedicates the first four hours he works each month to the bank to repay the borrowed funds. The bank acquires $1,600 of Matrix's future earnings or Time as compensation for lending him the money.

Here's another example: Matrix purchases a house with a thirty-year mortgage. Essentially, Matrix agrees to work for the bank for five workdays each month (equivalent to the mortgage payment) or sixty days a year for the next thirty years. Matrix has committed 1,800 days of future Time to the bank.

Borrowers can borrow from the future in short-term scenarios, like a credit card that gets paid off quickly, or the long term, such as a thirty-year mortgage obligation. Sometimes, borrowers secure future commitments by promising to repay them, which tends to incur high costs. In other cases, it's completely secured by a savings account of stored Time, which is typically the least expensive option.

If you are a borrower, it's crucial to have the correct type of debt that fits your situation.

WHAT IS A SPENDER?

A spender is an individual who utilizes all their resources, whether it's their Time or active currency. Let's go back to Matrix's vacation. If Matrix pays off the credit card in full at the end of the month, we would classify Matrix as a spender.

Matrix doesn't need to borrow; however, Matrix does need to work to earn money. This money (active currency) is then exchanged for goods and services provided by others.

Matrix doesn't accumulate savings (Time) for later use in this spender lifestyle. Instead, Matrix spends what is earned almost immediately.

WHAT IS A LENDER?

This is someone who has savings (passive currency) and gives it to a borrower (the counterparty) so that the borrower can convert it to spend or invest as active currency. A lender does this in exchange for a bit of the borrower's future Time.

If Matrix puts Time into a bank savings account, this is lending the bank Time. The bank then lends it to other borrowers for their future Time, of which Matrix gets a share.

WHAT IS AN OWNER?

This person takes passive currency to build a product or service that saves or occupies other people's Time.

The blacksmith saved the baker Time. The baker saved the farmer Time. The saloon owner gave the blacksmith, the baker, and the farmer a relaxing place to go. Each was the owner of his own business.

Matrix does not own a business. Matrix earned money from the work he did for someone else, and they paid him for the hours worked.

The clock controls Matrix's income.

Matrix's work situation is like that of most people across the country. A recent summary by the Pew Research Center indicated that of the 157 million people in the workforce in the United States, only about 16 million are self-employed.[37]

There are likely few business owners because owning a business is hard and risky. Indeed, according to the Small Business Administration's Office of Advocacy:

> From 1994 to 2019, an average of 67.6% of new employer establishments survived at least two years. During the same period, the five-year survival rate was 48.9%, the ten-year survival rate was 33.6%, and the fifteen-year survival rate was 25.7%.[38]

More succinctly, over 50 percent of new businesses fail for one reason or another within five years.

The question this raises is how the other 140 million people whose Time is controlled by the clock get a share of other people's Time.

They do this by understanding how the Time-Wealth Matrix works.

"The only difference between a rich person and a poor person is how they use their time."

—Robert Kiyosaki

TAKEAWAYS

Investing, when boiled down to its essence, is surprisingly straightforward. It's about deploying the excess time you've earned—your hard-earned resources—into the hands of a counterparty. In exchange, this counterparty promises to give back your time with a bonus. The bonus varies: interest if you're lending, dividends and growth if you're in ownership.

The heart of investing lies in identifying those counterparties capable of generating sufficient value from their products or services. This ability to generate value ensures you not only get your initial investment back but also reap additional returns, effectively doubling your money over time, guided by the Rule of 72. It's a balancing act of assessing risk and potential reward.

Understanding your capital structure is crucial in navigating this landscape. At various points, you might play the roles of borrower, spender, lender, and owner, sometimes simultaneously. This multifaceted financial existence demands a keen understanding of how to allocate your current and future resources. It's about leveraging time, not just your own but also that of others, to align with your goals and values. In this way, investing becomes not just a financial activity but a strategic approach to managing and growing your wealth over time.

CHAPTER 5

THE MONEY MATRIX ISN'T WHAT YOU THINK IT IS

THE TIME-WEALTH MATRIX

The Matrix is an action film that depicts the world as a simulation where a supercomputer controls the inhabitants' simulated reality. When Neo, the hero, learns how his world truly works, he trains his mind to control the simulation, his interactions with it, and ultimately bends the simulation to his will. Though, like all good movies, he struggles to overcome the obstacles put before him.

The Time-Wealth Matrix is not as exciting as an action movie, but there is one parallel. The supercomputer we call our mind controls our reality, present, and future. Besides the real-world obstacles of balancing the variables of the Wealth Equation, we also need an understanding of how to program this computer so we can manipulate it according to our will.

Understanding how our mind perceives past and future time and how it influences our choices will empower us to utilize the Time we accumulate more effectively. This will lead to genuine wealth creation.

We must also understand how our mind may take shortcuts to lead us in the wrong direction in a postindustrial era that kept our early ancestors alive as they were discovering fire and the wheel.

THE PERSONALITY LAYER OR
BALANCED TIME PERSPECTIVE

Time cannot be seen or felt directly and might be better described as a series of events. How we perceive those events begins to hardcode our personalities. This coding in turn, drives our interactions with future events.

Psychologists have studied how people adapt to events and have developed several time-based personality types to describe these adaptations.[39] I have met or worked with all these personalities over the last thirty years and outline them as follows:

- Past Positive: The Nostalgic—I have an older friend; when you hop in his car, you will only hear Motown or the Beach Boys' music. He has his golf ball from his hole-in-one and friends that go back to childhood. This personality type focuses on the "good old days."
- Past Negative: The Skeptic—I work with a few folks who are deeply afraid of a market meltdown. Their formative investment experience in the market was the technology crash of the early 2000s. This pessimistic personality type focuses on the past, thinking of themselves as realists. This personality type focuses on what went wrong in the past.

- Present Hedonistic: The YOLO Advocate—I have a client quickly running through inherited money who, after suffering through recent tragedies, is using the money to escape the pain they lived through over the past several years. This personality type has a live-in-the-moment approach to life.
- Present Fatalistic: The Resigned—I have helped folks who have a sense of despair over their financial future and feel they have no control. Typically, it was due to a series of unlikely events, a car accident, or job loss, and they now live with a general feeling of foreboding. This personality type feels their life is predetermined.
- Future-Oriented: The Planner—I enjoy working with this personality type as an advisor. They trust in their decisions and plan for the future. Unfortunately, this is also the type to become workaholics to save for the future, to the detriment of other parts of their lives. This personality type is always thinking ahead.
- Transcendental Future: The Spiritualist—I have clients who are very involved in their faith. They live their lives and have arranged their affairs in a manner very much geared to preparing for what comes next. This personality type focuses on life after death.

Thankfully, most of us do not fall solely into just one of these personality types; instead, we can navigate between them based on the circumstances.

I have found, and research shows, that individuals who balance past positive, present hedonistic, and future orientations tend to have more successful wealth outcomes.[40] An overemphasis on any one of the categories, especially the negative or fatalistic ones, sabotages success.

I've also found that when people effectively use the other

tendencies of the past negative, present fatalistic, and transcendental future orientations in moderation, they seem able to handle the adversities the world dishes out more effectively.

I believe this is because they actively incorporate negative possibilities into their decision-making processes, understand the possible adverse outcomes, and prepare for them.

This is the balance that allows us to pivot when the situation changes.

One's time perspective impacts all corners of wealth accumulation. Psychiatrists have cataloged this, and in my role as a financial advisor, I've noticed that people who over-emphasize negative perspectives might have the following symptoms:

- Money Avoidance
  - Financial Denial—Ignoring money issues instead of facing them, like avoiding bank statements or credit card bills.
  - Financial Rejection—Feeling guilty about having money. This can lead to deeper financial and psychological problems.
- Money-Worshipping
  - Hoarding—Collecting objects or money for a false sense of security and anxiety relief.
  - Compulsive Buying—Excessive spending driven by worries, often learned as a coping mechanism to escape anxiety.
- Relational Money
  - Financial Infidelity—Dishonestly spending money without a partner's knowledge, even big-ticket items or secret accounts.
  - Financial Enabling—Giving money despite affordability, sacrificing one's financial well-being for others, often seen in families during tough economic times.[41]

Understanding the base layer that all decisions about the future are built on will assist in making better decisions about the future.

Like all computer programs, if there is a bug in the code, many times it can be trapped and fixed by looking at past output. Do we make good choices based on what we know with little regret?

If not, sometimes we can easily correct this by quietly reflecting on our past and making changes that enable us to make better decisions with this understanding of ourselves in the future.

However, occasionally, the trauma that leads us to an unbalanced time perspective is so extreme or deep that we need professional help to overcome it. Things such as car accidents, natural disasters, physical abuse, and combat are difficult to overcome on our own, and seeking help is generally just an email or phone call away. Resources that are available, include:

- Employee assistance programs at work
- Ask your primary care provider for a referral
- PsychologyToday.com offers an online resource

The personality layer is the base layer of the Time-Wealth Matrix.

"The more you know who you are, and what you want, the less you let things upset you."

—Stephanie Perkins

COGNITIVE BIASES

Once we grasp the personality base layer, the next level of the matrix is to navigate the societal biases that helped our ancestors survive. In a world where time was controlled by the sun, these cognitive biases were critical to survival.

For example, if you lived in prehistoric times and everyone in your tribe was running in one direction, it was probably safer to run with them than try to determine why they were running. This is known as herd mentality and probably kept a fair number of humans from being devoured by predators.

However, in a world controlled by the clock, we must understand these cognitive biases to build wealth over time successfully.

People always use rules of thumb or mental shortcuts to make decisions. These are called heuristics (pronounced "you-ris-tics"). While heuristics help us make quick decisions, they do not always help us make the best decisions. Buster Benson has done the world a great service by compiling 175 cognitive biases into an organized list. *Medium* posted this "Cognitive Bias Cheat Sheet."[42]

At the highest level, these biases help us solve four basic problems:

- Too much information—The world is no longer constrained by the movement of the seasons. We are constantly bombarded with data, so the brain needs a shortcut to filter it all.
- Not enough meaning—With all this information and the need to filter it, the brain takes over and adds things and fills in the space with memories and previous experiences.
- The need to act fast—All of this is coming at us in real time, and we need to decide. Yellow traffic light: Should I run the light? Is it raining or snowy? Is it late or rush hour? Am I in the country or the city?

- What we should remember—The brain self-sorts its memories to keep the things that probably help with the first three problems on the list: generalizations about the world but specifics for our day-to-day lives.

But like all tools, they only solve problems if they are properly used for the right job. Here are the tools to be aware of in the context of building wealth:

How the mind handles too much information:

- Availability bias—Powerful memories overwhelm and make them seem more relevant, even when they do not apply. Memories of lottery commercials showing how easy it is to win may influence someone, even though the odds of winning are pretty low.
- Confirmation bias—People tend to favor information that affirms their preexisting beliefs and ignore or discount information that contradicts these beliefs. We also tend to seek evidence supporting our viewpoints and dismiss evidence contradicting it.
- Narrow framing—Individuals make decisions based on limited or narrow sets of potential outcomes, neglecting the relevant, broader context. This can result in overly cautious or risky choices, as the full scope of consequences or implications isn't considered.

How the mind handles not enough meaning:

- Recency bias—Excessive weight or importance is given to recent events or information while making judgments or decisions. It is characterized by the tendency to prioritize and rely more on the most recent or easily accessible information rather than considering a broader range of historical or long-term data.

- Bandwagon bias/herd mentality—Individuals adopt certain beliefs or behaviors because many others are doing the same. It is because people often conform to the actions and opinions of the majority to feel accepted or to avoid standing out.
- Mental accounting—Individuals often think about their finances in fragmented and subjective ways, rather than taking a holistic approach. By compartmentalizing assets, individuals make poor long-term choices.

How the mind handles the need to act fast:

- Loss aversion—We choose what in our minds is the least risky option or something that maintains the status quo.
- Overconfidence—We are overconfident in our abilities. Studies have shown that more than 70 percent of drivers think they are above average! This also flows through to investment decisions.

How the mind handles memory:

- Peak-end rule—People judge an experience largely based on how they felt at its most intense point (its peak) and at its end, rather than based on the total sum or average of every moment of the experience. The result of this is that a single moment of overwhelming joy or displeasure can greatly influence how we remember an entire event and shapes us in making future decisions.
- Misattribution of memory—Confusing the time, place, people, or details involved in a memory. This can lead to creating false memories or distorted perceptions of events.

We need shortcuts in today's world, but being aware of how these cognitive biases can lead us down the wrong path is critical for our future success.

RISK VERSUS PERCEIVED RISK

Some people will jump out of a plane with a parachute. Others would never voluntarily step out of an airplane while it is 8,000 feet in the air. However, almost everyone would drive a friend who wants to parachute for their fiftieth birthday to the airfield to be part of the event, even if they are keeping their feet on terra firma.

When a friend asks, most people will instantly make the jump/no-jump decision. But how was the risk decision made?

Risks of Dying:

- Skydiving, 1 in 101,083 jumps[43]
- Driving, 16 per 100,000 drivers[44]
- Most people don't know this information when they say yes or no to jumping from a plane, but not knowing does not stop one from deciding. This example illustrates the following problems.
  - Too much information—The availability bias means one is more likely to remember a failed parachutist's spectacular story than an automobile accident's typical story. To thoroughly compare the two, we must understand the relationship between jumpers and drivers.
  - Not enough meaning—The bandwagon bias simplifies all this math to a simple jump/no-jump decision to balance the risk of driving versus jumping versus staying home based on the understanding that most people don't jump out of airplanes.

- Need to act fast—Loss aversion bias might consider the dollar cost of the adventure and the risk of dying to say yes or no quickly.

While all this is going on, the personality gets a vote in the decision-making process, including present hedonistic or fatalistic orientations, introversion or extroversion, and life experiences.

In a rational world, everyone would make consistent decisions based on the level of risk involved. However, the fact that some people are willing to leap from airplanes while others won't even consider it shows that risk perception varies greatly among individuals.

These individual risk perceptions and cognitive biases shape our decisions in various aspects of life, whether it's socializing with new people, going on trips with friends, relocating to a new city, accepting a job promotion, changing careers, purchasing a vehicle, investing, or making any other daily decision.[45]

TIME VERSUS PERCEIVED TIME

I recently relearned that a clock at sea level moves slower than a clock at the top of a mountain.[46] Gravity warps space and time, causing time to move differently. While science has proven this, a person climbing a mountain would never notice the difference.

But what is noticed is that, like a clock at sea level, a child subjectively perceives time as moving slower than how their parents and grandparents subjectively perceive time. One study suggests this difference in perception is in proportion to the square root of the perceiver's real age. This subjective perception is outlined in the chart below.

Subjective Acceleration of Time with Aging

Age	10	20	40	60	80	100
10	1.0	1.4	2.0	2.4	2.8	3.2
20		1.0	1.4	1.7	2.0	2.2
40			1.0	1.2	1.4	1.6
60				1.0	1.2	1.3
80					1.0	1.1
100						1.0

Reading across the top, this means a sixty-year-old would subjectively experience time passing 2.4 times more quickly than a ten-year-old, 1.7 times more quickly than a twenty-year-old and 1.2 times faster than a forty-year-old. While a person who is age eighty experiences time two times faster than a twenty-year-old.[47]

As we look at a lifetime, this might explain why the last third seems to fly by three times faster than the first. This is probably why our parents and grandparents always ask where time has gone, while our young children never do.

Additionally, we've all experienced time seemingly disappearing while reading, watching a movie, or working on an engaging project. We perceive this even though we know time did not speed up or slow down.

Finally, time has a cultural element.

China is often credited with thinking in one hundred-year terms, while the US tends to think in election cycles.[48] I am not sure this is true, but anthropologist Edward T. Hall has offered that societies perceive the future in one of two ways:[49]

- Monochronic perception places emphasis on the linear perception of time. Time is segmented and precise. It can be arranged and scheduled and is a commodity.
- Polychronic perception places emphasis on a holistic and synchronous perception of time. Time is flexible and open and sets the context for something to happen, so time is less valued than the relationships it triggers.

Societies, communities, and businesses don't have a uniform perspective on the future, and no two individuals perceive time exactly the same way.

Eminent minds such as Aristotle, Newton, and Einstein have all presented their thoughts on time, and their theories have been subject to discussion and interpretation for centuries or even millennia. Physicists quantify time in terms of Planck time (I would define this if I understood this), while psychologists develop theories surrounding our perceptions of time.

This divergence regarding what time is tells us that time is a subjective experience that varies among individuals. Our past and present significantly influence our attitudes, emotions, and choices about the future. The accumulation of wealth of any kind necessitates the investment of Time, whether ours or someone else's.

Every individual's perception and allocation of their present, future, and accumulated Time reveals their core values.

THE TIME-WEALTH MATRIX

The Time-Wealth Matrix is a tool that allows one to better allocate their Time in all its forms based on their perceived risk level. A person's matrix matches perfectly to their personal perceptions of risk and time. Like a well-tailored suit or dress, our matrix may be similar to another's, but it is custom to us.

Remember,

- Skill × Time = Value
  - This value can be spent currently, or the Time component can be stripped off and stored.
  - Society assigns different values to different skills. While a farmer's and blacksmith's skills may be about equal in value, society values Taylor Swift's singing skills significantly higher than practically any other artist on the planet.
  - An hour of Taylor's time is not more important than anyone else's. However, Taylor's personal matrix may value that hour differently than others might. She might hire a chef to cook her meals so she can make more appearances with her time. In contrast, most of us would just go to the diner down the street since no one wants to hear us sing. (More precisely, no one wants to hear me sing!)
- Perceived Risk = Jump/No-Jump
  - Our mind values every decision based on our cognitive biases, personality traits, and the perceived cost of stored, current, and future Time.
- Future Time = A Lot/A Little
  - We each have a limited amount of future Time, and we each value our remaining futures differently. All decisions regarding the use of this future Time require that we allocate a lot or a little of this precious asset to a decision.

Plotting your personal Time-Wealth Matrix might look like this:

- A lottery ticket—Most folks properly perceive this as a high-risk event for which a person should only spend a small amount of Time and value.
  - The Mega-Millions—Bet $1 and get the chance to win $1 billion next Wednesday.
- A new home—Most folks properly perceive this as a low-risk event requiring significant Time and value.
  - Parents find a home in the neighborhood where they want to raise their children and commute to work for the next twenty years. They borrow for thirty years and use up a significant amount of money/stored Time as a down payment.

Most people will not allocate a whole paycheck to buying lottery tickets, nor would they buy a house in a sketchy neighborhood with a long commute to work.

But some people do.

They will do this because their cognitive biases result in balancing the equation of perceived risk with the use of stored and future Time differently than most, leading them to a decision with a low probability of success.

Everyone's Time-Wealth Matrix, like the Wealth Equation, is personalized based on the individual's perceived risk, stored Time/money, and how they perceive future Time availability.

Most would plot the location of lottery tickets, cash, and real estate on a graph and say the following graph seems in balance:

Time-Wealth Matrix

Stored Time (money)

Perceived Risk		Immediate	Short-Term	Medium-Term	Long-Term	Very Long-Term	Generational
8	Unknown						
7	Extreme						
6	Very High	Buying a lottery ticket					
5	High						
4	Above Average						
3	Moderate						
2	Low						
1	Very Low	Putting money in a savings account					Building a house in the town you grew up in

Future Time

(Stored Time axis: Little → Lots)

Again, most see a lottery ticket as a high-risk event. Most would not buy one if they needed to hold it for five years, waiting for their number to be called. Few would consider selling all they had to acquire a ticket, but some would.

Similarly, most see a new home purchase as an expensive decision they will put significant Time and money into.

As we work on creating our personal Time-Wealth Matrix, things become more intricate. It's important to remember that wealth extends beyond cash, lottery tickets, and homes.

Each individual's perception of risk varies, as does their concept of the future and what they consider valuable in terms of stored Time (passive currency). All purchases come with an opportunity cost that we consciously or unconsciously compare to the other options.

We must balance this use of Time with the perceived risk associated with the activity or item in question.

An example is getting a child into Harvard. Some parents will devote nights and weekends to tutoring their children and spend hundreds of thousands of dollars to send them to the best schools, all for the chance to be competitive in the college admissions process. In this situation, the perceived risk of the child receiving anything less than what they perceive is the best education possible is worth the expenditure of both future and stored Time/money.

Other parents might consider the requirements to get into Harvard and perceive the risk of not allowing their child to spend more Time in sports and social activities to be more significant than what college their child might attend.

Time-Wealth Matrix

Stored Time (money) — Little → Lots

Perceived Risk		Immediate	Short-Term	Medium-Term	Long-Term	Very Long-Term	Generational
Unknown	8	Sampling a mysterious beverage	Bungee jumping				Starting a business
Extreme	7	Trying street food in an unfamiliar region	Adventure travel to top of mountain or bottom of ocean			Investing in a friend's unproven business idea	Investing in futuristic but unproven tech
Very High	6	Buying a lottery ticket	Joining a high-stakes poker game				Sailing around the world with the family
High	5	Playing a slot machine		Investing in cryptocurrency	Opening a franchise		Purchasing artwork for inheritance
Above Average	4	Betting on a sports game			Investing in a startup	Renovating an old property in a known area	Emigrating to a new country
Moderate	3	Trying a new local restaurant	Learning a new hobby		Buying stocks	Investing in child's education	Buying land for future generations
Low	2		Buying a car	Buying energy-efficient appliances	Buying government bonds	Purchasing life insurance	
Very Low	1	Putting money in a savings account			Getting married and having children	Saving in a retirement plan over a career	Building a house in the town you grew up in

Future Time

The choices are endless, but they are for each individual or family to make.

This person puts a startup business as a high-risk event they would expect to spend a significant Time on but would invest little money into because of the risk of loss. However, serial entrepreneurs might view the same business as a low-risk opportunity for which they can delegate operations and invest substantial amounts of money, anticipating a higher return.

The goal of the Time-Wealth Matrix is to provide a framework to compare these decisions. We will get to more concrete techniques in a later chapter.

Keep in mind, though, that each decision balances these three variables. Each decision our present selves make is a new path to our future selves, and every decision after that does the same.

"We see the world not as it is, but as we are."

—STEPHEN COVEY

TAKEAWAYS

Understanding the interaction between our minds and the world is a crucial skill to master.

Cognitive biases greatly impact how we perceive time and risk, making them essential elements in developing our personal Time-Wealth Matrix. By recognizing how past experiences shape our biases and influence our decisions, we can better comprehend why our perspectives differ from others and can help us make more informed choices.

Finally, we become empowered to make wealth-related decisions that align with our long-term interests by being conscious of how our chronological age and the cultures we were raised in affect our perceptions of time.

With this understanding of Time, our personal history, and our biases in check, let's hack this matrix.

PART TWO

EXECUTION

Here we are in Mexico, having the time of our lives, crossing desert flats, pushing the cars to the max, and at the end of the first day, drinking cerveza, swapping stories, and eating authentic Mexican cuisine.

Early on the second day, the dust and rocks are so nasty our Baja cars have spaced out about a mile apart to maintain visibility. We're third in line, cruising at a steady fifty, when the radio crackles to life: "Leader, we have a problem." "What's that?" "Uhm, we're upside down."

And that's how fast life happens.

We would drive for miles and suddenly experience the highest thrills, only to be followed a few miles later by fear and worry.

Over the course of those few days of racing across the desert, we had cars upside down, crashing into ravines, stuck in the sand flats, and on railroad tracks.

But by design, they built the cars and protective equipment for just such a trip. The guide, having run this route before, had back-up contingencies and support for just about anything that could happen, and with this crew of drivers, he had to use most of them!

This journey through Baja reflects the broader journey of life—moments of smooth cruising punctuated by joyful but life-altering events. A wedding, a birth, a dream job. Then out of the blue, the phone rings late at night, and you hear, "Uhm, I hate to be the one to tell you this, but…" and your whole world turns upside down.

In Part Two, you navigate your life, knowing you can bend the future to your will, even though it is unknowable. While your life path and experiences are unique, you can plan in advance for the well-trodden landscape you are traveling through and the horizon you are heading to.

However, remember the words from our guide: "This isn't Disney World, and there is no rail to keep you on the track."

"Prepare for the unknown by studying how others in the past have coped with unforeseeable and the unpredictable."

—GEORGE S. PATTON

CHAPTER 6

PUTTING THE PIECES TOGETHER

The only way to hack a system is to understand its parts. Once we know how the system runs, we figure out how to get around the obstacles blocking us from getting things done.

A quick review is in order.

- Time—We experience Time over our lives as a depleting asset that seems to move faster as we age and have less of it.
- Skill—This a combination of experience, knowledge, and wisdom. Some skills are more valued than others by society.
- Skill × Time = Work.
- Work creates Value.
- Value—In a barter system, value is traded for value, such as wheat for bread. When barter breaks down, governments introduce currency to ease trade.
- Currency—In a banking system, currency represents value (e.g., denarius for wheat, bread, and ovens). It works because

everyone agrees on the currency's value for trade. Currency has no intrinsic value.

- Active currency—This is given to others for current services (e.g., ironworks for bread) or Time savings (e.g., new ovens that bake more bread).
- Passive currency—This is stored Time, and the act of creating it allows the owner to replace earnings from work or build wealth over time.
- Stored Time—This can be lent or invested. An owner of stored Time can lend it to someone else, such as the banker or the miller, or they can buy a future income stream by investing in a business as an owner.
- Lending—An owner of stored Time can lend directly to a borrower or combine with others to diversify the lending with a bond. The borrower is the person who encumbers their future Time/money to purchase something in the present. The borrower is the lender's counterparty. The lender earns interest.
- Interest—This is the future Time/money of the borrower they give to the lender for being able to spend money today.
- Owner—The owner of stored Time can invest in entities that will generate future profits. Shareholders receive a portion of the profits based on their stock ownership percentage.
- Stock—This is shareholder ownership interest in a business that offers customers value in exchange for their active or stored Time. When the business income exceeds its costs, this is a profit.
- Profit—This is other people's Time. After a business pays its suppliers and employees, this Time is distributed to the owners as dividends based on their shareholder percentage of ownership. Each company stock has a different price or value based on its level of perceived risk.

- Perceived risk—This is the jump/no-jump decision based on each person's time perspective, cognitive biases, and stored and future Time commitments.
- Future Time—This is each individual's perceived Time left in their lifetime.
- Wealth—This is an abundance of family, friends, experiences, knowledge, wisdom, material objects, financial resources, and Time.

The world is an interrelated and complicated place. There are billions of people making trillions of decisions moving toward their futures. But each one of these decisions, no matter how mundane, incorporates Time, risk, personality, and cultural biases into the equation.

Understanding and incorporating this into the process allows one to make better decisions for themselves and their loved ones.

YOUR WEALTH ERA

In *The Order of Time*, quantum physicist Carlo Rovelli expresses a great thought about our time here on Earth. He says,

> The best grammar for thinking of the world is that of change, not permanence, not of being but becoming.[50]

Becoming what?

Hacking the Time-Wealth Matrix can help guide us to an answer. However, with endless potential timelines unfolding before us, achieving success requires certain boundaries to make the process practicable.

The initial boundary is Time.

During the lifetime they are given, people will grow, learn, work, make friends, establish families, retire, explore, and eventually transition to whatever or wherever they believe awaits beyond this life.

I term this block of Time your Personal Era of Wealth.

I call it this because, like the overlapping eras from history, such as the Victorian (1820–1914) and Progressive eras (1896–1917), it is the collective decisions of the society we live in and that preceded us that define our era. Similarly, our parent's decisions and choices impact our outlook on the world, as our decisions and choices impact our children and grandchildren.

The ripples of our decisions will continue outward over time to multiple generations.

I see this when I meet with clients whose families helped them with the down payment on a home, a college tuition payment, or just emotional support in a trying time. One of my favorite stories is about an uncle who left his modest estate directly to his niece through his will. Several years after his passing, this inheritance allowed the niece to provide a specialized education program for her troubled teenage child, who, because of this gift, has now graduated with honors from college and has a bright future. Without this unexpected gift, the outcome would have been very different.

The choices we make have an impact for generations to come. We still discuss the Kennedy's political legacy, Carnegie's lending libraries, and the Walton Family charitable foundation.

While you are probably not a billionaire, your Era of Wealth will still outlast you. However, your direct impact on your era, like Joe Kennedy, Andrew Carnegie, and Sam Walton, is constrained by your lifetime. A lifetime is unknowable for each person, but it needs to be constrained as a variable. I define a lifetime as lasting ninety-nine years.

NINETY-NINE YEARS IS NOT THAT LONG A TIME

Ninety-nine years isn't unrealistic in today's world. The number of people living past one hundred has been increasing for decades. A study from the University of Washington found that the odds of living past 110 are becoming more likely.[51]

In working with my clients, I understand that the risk of depleting wealth of all types is a long life, not a short one.

Indeed, one of my clients, who was a widow of ninety-three at the time, told me, "Pat, I never expected to live this long." Her worry was running out of money.

We got her through, and she left funds to the next generation at her passing at age ninety-five. This is because our planning assumes a long life, though some clients laugh at us and say bluntly, "Age ninety-five? That's never going to happen."

Also, across my years in personal finance, I have noticed that people live their Era of Wealth in three epochs or stages.

THE THREE EPOCHS OF WEALTH
THAT DEFINE YOUR ERA

In our journey through life, we encounter distinct epochs, each marked by a gradual evolution that guides us into subsequent phases.

As eloquently described by Rovelli, we are not merely existing but continuously evolving.

I describe these epochs as:

1. Learning and Base Building—A time for acquiring knowledge and establishing foundational skills.
2. Protection and Accumulation—A period focused on safeguarding and building upon what we've learned and acquired.

3. Withdrawing/Passing Time—A phase of reflection, withdrawal, and imparting wisdom to others.

Now it is time to dive deeper into understanding these transformative phases and how they shape our life's trajectory.

"The biggest adventure you can take is to live the life of your dreams."
—Oprah Winfrey

CHAPTER 7

EPOCH I: LEARNING AND BASE-BUILDING— BIRTH TO AGE THIRTY-THREE

It is thought we are born into the world with nothing. I could not disagree more. We are born with wealth beyond all imagination.

Having seen a mother's love for her child and having held my sons, Ryan and Russell, mere minutes after their birth, along with my grandsons O and K right after theirs, I understand. We start with family. I see this also when I talk to new moms and dads worried about college costs and grandparents trying to figure out what their role is in helping this new family.

While not every child is born into the perfect family, in general, these new lives possess a remarkable abundance of family. Parents, obviously, but uncles and aunts can't wait to see and hold them. People step up and pledge their assets to care for them if something happens to the parents. Grandparents cannot stop bragging about them—well, I can't anyway!

They are also born with an asset that everyone wishes they had more of: Time.

On their balance sheet, a child has two major assets: Time and family.

Time we have defined as ninety-nine years. This newborn also has their parents' Time, which I estimate at sixty years.

Wealth Era — Day 1

Account	Asset	Liability
Parents	60	0
Siblings	0	0
Time	<u>99</u>	<u>0</u>
Total	159	0
Net Worth		**159**

In the classic board game Monopoly, the banker gives everyone $1,500 to start with. In the same way, we all begin with our own resources: Time, our parents, and ourselves. As we navigate life, we encounter positive and negative events, much like the difficulties of moving around the Monopoly board.

Understanding the rules of this multigenerational game of wealth creation is critical to our success, as we must learn to use them to our advantage. Our choices will shape our futures, so let's hack the game where we can!

While everyone grows up at a different rate, childhood starts when we are born and winds down around age eighteen. This stage is broken into three parts, and children should begin to learn about Time, value, money, and currency in progressively more complex terms during each phase.[52]

- Early Childhood (Birth to Eight Years)
  - This time frame is marked by skill development (e.g., motor skills, language, and personality)
  - Items to Learn:
    - Understanding currency—what it is used for, where to use it, who prints it
    - Needs and wants
    - Saving and spending
    - Borrowing and lending
- Middle Childhood (Eight to Twelve Years)
  - Interpersonal and social relationship competencies are acquired.
  - By age eight, children understand time and money.
  - Items to Learn:
    - Buying decisions
    - Budgeting and payment options
    - Savings
    - Charitable giving
    - How value is created—jobs and careers
- Adolescence (Twelve to Eighteen Years)
  - Individuals think and reason about problems and ideas.
  - By eighteen, individuals understand death. They have been exposed to it through culture, religion, and perhaps personal experience.

- Teenagers are estimated to spend about $63 billion annually in the United States.[53]
- Items to Learn—Progressively more complex understandings of:
  - Earning—Job and career requirements
  - Spending—Needs, wants, consumerism
  - Saving and investing—How to accumulate assets
  - Borrowing—Credit, Time, costs
  - Protecting—Identity, money, credit, and trusted counterparties

The concepts of wealth are abstract, but children will learn them by watching their parents, family, friends, and television, and by browsing the internet.

It is safe to say that many of these lessons are taught by people who do not understand wealth themselves or are purposely trying to catch your children's attention. It is also unlikely the education system will provide quality information to our children healthily.

Only twenty-five states require a course in economics to graduate, and only twenty-three require a student to take a personal finance class.[54] Perhaps more importantly, while 67 percent of teachers believe financial education should start in elementary school, only 31 percent feel entirely comfortable teaching financial education.[55]

Children who learn about Time, money, and currency become self-sufficient. Helping them develop a healthy relationship with how value is created and stored and the reasons for spending it will be invaluable as they walk through life.

By age eighteen, most cultures and laws consider a person an adult.

However, anyone who has lived through it knows there is

still a long way to go. Millennials have even coined a word for it: adulting. This refers to people over eighteen who "adult" less than 50 percent of the time.

Regardless, they have the basic education that society says is enough to move forward in the world—a high school education. As a result, every high school graduate has a big decision to make.

HACK #1—TEACH KIDS ABOUT TIME, MONEY, AND CURRENCY

DECISION TIME—GO TO WORK OR GO TO COLLEGE

Is college worth it?

If, like many of my clients, a parent's goal is to top off and round out their children's education and provide them with better critical thinking skills and experiences, then the answer to the question is yes.

However, if the goal is simply to get a better job, then let's define this decision a little better.

According to the Manhattan Institute, there's a trend in earnings based on educational attainment.[56] They found that students who graduated in the top half of their high school class but didn't attend college earned about the same as college graduates who finished in the bottom half of their class.

Even more notable is that high-school-only graduates in the top 25 percent of their class tended to out-earn those who graduated in the bottom 25 percent of their college class. This suggests that academic performance in high school can be a significant factor in future earnings, even without a college degree.

Unlike in Garrison Keillor's whimsical stories of Lake Wobegon, all the children going to college are not above average.

The averages are made up of real people living real lives and doing real things, and not all will earn above-average wages. In this world, 50 percent of the folks going to college to improve their job prospects made the wrong decision. Additionally, the statistics from the Manhattan Institute jibe with other statistics indicating that about 45 percent of recent college grads said they work at jobs that do not require a college degree.[57]

Whether a college degree is worth it depends on each student, their course of study, whether they have to borrow to pay tuition, and if a degree is the best path for success in their chosen field. The answers are beyond the scope of this book.

I will instead approach these questions from a wealth-hack angle. And this means, for an eighteen-year-old, it is about future Time.

First, what does the short-term future hold for high school and college graduates?

PriceWaterhouseCoopers[58] and the University of Oxford[59] predict that between 38 percent and 47 percent of jobs are at high risk of automation. This next wave of automation is coming for transportation, retail, clerical, and accounting jobs.

As a result, regardless of their educational attainment, all students should be aware of this trend and work toward learning skills that a robot cannot take over.

Whether they decide to earn a college degree, everyone must go out and make their way in the world. Based on median incomes, the higher the level of education, the higher the median income. According to Northeastern University's average salary level by education estimates,[60] the median annual income is as follows:

- High school diploma: $42,081
- Bachelor's degree: $69,381
- Master's degree: $81,867

But using this as a starting point is like beginning to read *Moby Dick* in a middle chapter. Who is this guy named Ahab, and why is he chasing a white whale? Obviously, we have missed a lot of the storyline.

The Time-Wealth Matrix storyline revolves around Time and money as our main characters. It takes considerable Time, money, and effort to qualify for these median income levels. For instance, obtaining a bachelor's degree takes four years and costs approximately $100,000 for college graduates.[61] Pursuing a master's degree adds two years and $100,000 to the total cost.[62]

A different way of looking at Northeastern's salary results might look like this:

- High school diploma: $42,081, opportunity cost $0 and zero years
- Bachelor's degree: $69,381, opportunity cost $100,000 and four years
- Master's degree: $81,867, opportunity cost $200,000 and six years

Graphically, that looks something like this, where the trades go right to work, the bachelor goes to school for four years, and the master goes for six.

Trades — Start Work after High School

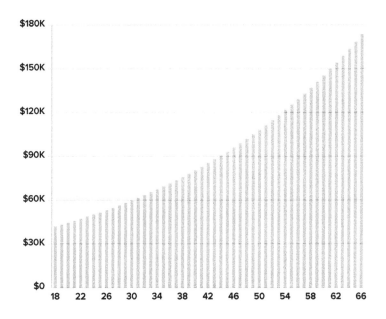

Bachelor — Begin Work after 4 Years and Paying for College

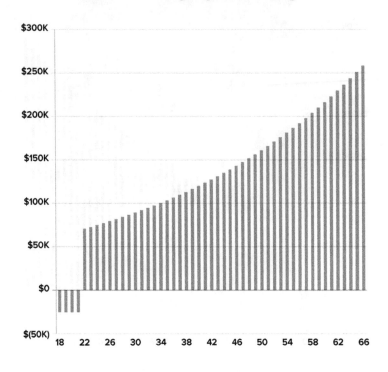

Master's — Begin Work after 6 Years and Paying for College

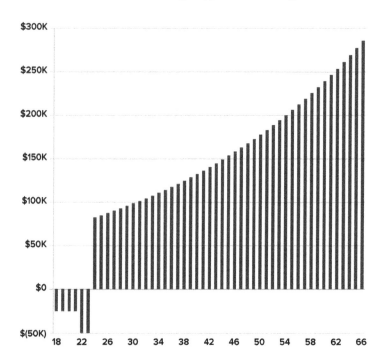

To keep this example simple, let's assume they all start working at the median salaries listed above, get an annual raise of 3 percent, and save 10 percent of their income. At age sixty-six, they will make the following:

- Trades: $173,000 per year
- Bachelor's: $254,000 per year
- Master's: $283,000 per year

These incomes are as you would expect, given their educations. Let's compare a lifetime of earnings at age sixty-six:

- Trades: $4.5 million
- Bachelor's: $6.3 million
- Master's: $6.7 million

This income difference is also as you would expect, given their degrees.

But to hack the matrix, you must understand how to compare things accurately, and in this simple example, Time makes all the difference. Remember, the trades start making money right out of high school. The folks getting degrees have to wait four or six years.

If you are of a certain age, you will remember the famous quote by J. Wellington Wimpy from the comic strip *Popeye*:

I'll gladly pay you Tuesday for a hamburger today.

What is more valuable to Wimpy, the hamburger today or the payment on Tuesday?

In finance, we would use a mathematical formula called Present Value to compare the value of a hamburger today versus the future payment on Tuesday. More precisely, Present Value compares different income streams paid over varying time frames. If I earn 7 percent on my money then, getting $1,000 in ten years is worth $508 today. It also shows us that ten payments of $1,000 is equal to $7,089 today or the Present Value of the income stream.

Receiving 10 payments of $1,000 over time...										
Today's Value	Today	Year 2	Year 3	Year 4	Year 5	Year 6	Year 7	Year 8	Year 9	Year 10
$1,000	$1,000	$1,000	$1,000	$1,000	$1,000	$1,000	$1,000	$1,000	$1,000	$1,000
$873										
$816										
$763										
$713										
$667										
$623										
$582										
$544										
$508										
$7,089	...is the same as receiving $7,089 today.									

This Time Value of money calculation shows us the worth of our future income stream, starting at age eighteen, including the cost of college, if we received it as a lump sum today.

Several calculations are associated with the Time Value of money: present value, future value, net present value, and others. While the calculations are interesting to math geeks, most financial calculators can do the math quicker and easier.

If we were to find someone to write those checks, each person would receive a different amount:

- Trades would get $576,070.
- Bachelor's degree holders would get $562,605.
- Master's degree holders would get $482,589.

This may seem surprising, but we should remember that the college students in this example had several years of negative cash flow early in the calculation. These payments significantly impact the value of their lifetime income streams because a dollar spent at age eighteen (the hamburger today) is way more valuable than a dollar received at age sixty-six (pay you on Tuesday).

It's also important to remember this is just an academic exercise since no one will write that check before someone does the work. The more crucial real-life question is: "Who gets to $1,000,000 of savings first?"

Based on my experience, most people can allocate 10 percent of their income to pay off debt or to save for investments.

In this example, two of our graduates need to use 10 percent of their incomes first to repay the cost of college. Then, once college repayments are done, they save to an account to earn a 10 percent return on their investments. Finally, everyone's salaries and the corresponding amount saved increase by 3 percent per year.

The Race of Time to $1,000,000

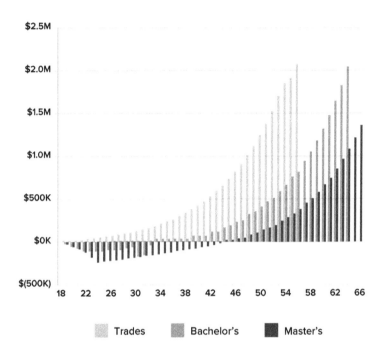

Given this, when will each of these savers reach $1,000,000 of accumulated Time?

- With no college to pay off, the high school graduate starts an apprenticeship right out of high school with 3 percent pay raises and 10 percent savings, so savings break down like this at age:
  - Eighteen—$4,200 of a $42,000 salary
  - Nineteen—$4,320 of a $43,250 salary
  - Twenty—$4,458 of the $44,580 salary
  - Twenty-one—$4,589 of the $45,890 salary
  - Given this savings pattern, this person reaches $1,000,000 in their late forties and $2,000,000 in their fifties.
- The second student graduates at age twenty-two, and their

income starts at $69,381. But they start life in the hole for the $100,000 of college cost, plus $20,314 (opportunity cost) that the first graduate has saved.

- ○ This person breaks even at age thirty-five and reaches $1,000,000 in their late fifties and $2,000,000 in their mid-sixties.
- The last student graduates at age twenty-four with a starting income of $81,867. They start life in the hole for $200,000 of college costs plus $43,131 that the high school graduate has saved.
  - ○ This person breaks even at age forty-four and reaches $1,000,000 in their mid-sixties.

Some would say, "My parents paid for this education, so I do not have to pay it back."

Well, what if they had invested the money for you at eighteen, and you didn't touch it until age forty-eight? Those funds would grow to be more than $1,000,000 over thirty years.

That is the opportunity cost of going to college.

An important note is this is a simple analysis; none of these choices are right or wrong. If we change our assumptions, the answers change too. However, if the goal is to create wealth, understand the rules of wealth creation:

- Opportunity costs
- Compounding
- Time Value of Money
  - ○ Present Value
  - ○ Future Value

We have graduated and have been working for a few years. This means we are about 80 percent of the way through the first epoch.

Other life events are unfolding between the ages of twenty-five and thirty-three:

- Experiences—Travel, vacations, promotions, on-the-job-training, job changes, career changes
- Family—Children arrive; according to the Centers for Disease Control and Prevention, for women the average is age twenty-six and for men thirty-one[63]
- Spouses—According to The Knot, the average age for a marriage is about thirty-one[64]
- Big purchases—Typical first-time home buyers are in their early to mid-thirties[65]

Life is moving fast, and perceived time is speeding up as we grow older. Friends are moving on and up, our families are expecting more from us, and relationships are becoming a bit more complicated.

There is a well-researched set of steps in the wealth progression that is proven to be effective in this learning and base-building phase.[66] It is called the "success sequence:"

1. Graduate—High school; 73 percent chance you avoid poverty in your thirties.
2. Full-time work—90 percent who graduate and work full time avoid poverty in their thirties.
3. Get married before kids—97 percent of people who do all three are able to avoid poverty in their thirties.

The Institute for Family Studies outlines this research by the Brookings Institute and others.[67] Details on each of these topics are beyond the scope of this book, but know, graduating, working full time, and being married before having children increase the odds of being wealthy and practically eliminates the likelihood of being poor.

To be ahead of your cohort though, hack the Matrix!

A lot has happened in the last thirty-two years, and as we approach the next epoch of protecting and accumulation, a quick review of our Time balance sheet is in order.

Wealth Era — End of Epoch I

Account	Asset	Liability
Parents	27	14
Siblings	66	33
Friends	66	33
Mentorships	0	5
Experiences	33	0
Knowledge	33	20
Wisdom	5	0
Things/Stuff	10	5
Financial Assets	1	0
Time	66	0
Total	307	110
Net Worth		197

Our balance sheet has improved over the first epoch. We should have picked up some knowledge, friends, experiences, stuff, and maybe a little wisdom.

The downside is that we have burned Time. We've depleted 33 percent of our Time asset, moving from ninety-nine years to sixty-six. We've also used up some family Time. Our parents are getting older, and our Time with them is running low.

We have also picked up liabilities. Financial liabilities include car loans, credit cards, and educational debt. Other liabilities are nonfinancial: our parents will need help soon—what is our responsibility to help them? Siblings and friends will likely need a shoulder, an ear, and perhaps a bit of our wallet in the future. We should plan to be there for them if they are there for us.

HACK #2—GRADUATE IN THE TOP 50 PERCENT, LEARN UN-ROBOTIZABLE SKILLS, SAVE 10 PERCENT OF YOUR INCOME, GET MARRIED, THEN HAVE KIDS

TAKEAWAYS

From a young age, we are taught the value of family, sharing, friendship, fairness, and napping. Yet, as we grow and progress through the education system, we are often pressured to conform to certain molds that are believed to lead to financial success.

However, true wealth can come in various forms, such as through the support of and for loved ones, meaningful experiences, and finding one's purpose. Teaching young individuals about essential concepts like skills, success systems, opportunity costs, and asset growth can have significant benefits in the long run as we navigate through the epochs ahead.

Learning these lessons about wealth is not easy in this epoch. While we have devoured reams of information, it has not coalesced into a lot of wisdom yet. Most are just trying to get ahead and are looking at the next class, the next raise, the next promotion, and the next job. They are being tactical when they should be strategic.

For those reading this who are already through this stage, look back and see if perhaps there is a young person in a new position who could use a mentor to make the path a little easier. Good karma tends to be returned!

"Thirty was so strange for me. I've really had to come to terms with the fact that I am now a walking and talking adult."

—C.S. Lewis

CHAPTER 8

EPOCH II: PROTECTION AND ACCUMULATION— AGE THIRTY-THREE TO AGE SIXTY-SIX

Congrats, you survived!

People tend to look back on their first epoch wistfully for the rest of their lives. This is probably because they make best friends, have first experiences, achieve independence, and make real decisions about the future based on real-life experiences.

It is also a time when some hard lessons are learned. By this time, most people have suffered serious losses. Losing grandparents and at least one parent is likely. Many have had a friend or coworker pass due to illness or accident. Most have made one or two bad financial decisions that have set them back.

Within this context, a new family and life are likely being

formed. Marriage and children then drive other decisions, such as where to live, what job makes sense, how many kids to have, and finally, what life will look like when this epoch ends.

Let's get to it. What is protecting and accumulating?

BAD THINGS HAPPEN TO GOOD PEOPLE

Bad things run the gambit from a little bad luck to soul-crushing events that people on the outside cannot fathom.

Over the past thirty years, I've seen clients go through minor inconveniences like flat tires and significant life changes, such as unexpected job losses. Unfortunately, I've also seen clients receive the devastating news of a terminal cancer diagnosis, leaving only days to settle personal affairs.

Thankfully, the likelihood of encountering a flat tire is far greater than that of receiving a terminal cancer diagnosis, though both remain within the realm of possibilities. However, their impacts differ significantly. A flat tire is a mere inconvenience, while a terminal diagnosis can be catastrophic for a family. The former might not warrant significant preventative measures, while the latter certainly does.

An insurance company's role is to pool the passive Time of many people in the form of insurance premiums. When a terrible event hits, this pool of Time provides the few people who need it Time in the form of currency.

For safeguarding your future, it's wise to delegate the less-probable yet potentially catastrophic risks to insurance companies while personally shouldering the more probable but lower impact risks. Let's take a closer look at some examples:

- An extended warranty on your computer monitor. While it may seem likely that your monitor could break at some point, the impact of such an event is relatively minor. It may be bothersome, but it won't significantly alter the course of your life. Probably not worth it.

- On the other hand, imagine being involved in an automobile accident that leaves you unable to work for a year. While this is a less probable occurrence, it has the potential to wreak havoc on both your personal and financial situations. Investing in appropriate insurance coverage is prudent to protect against this devastating scenario.

By strategically distributing the burden of risk, you can ensure that you are prepared for both the unexpected calamities that could upend your life and the more commonplace inconveniences that may arise.

SIGNIFICANT RISKS TO INSURE AGAINST

Loss of income is typically the first domino that tips us into a spiral of events that destroys all of one's wealth. Remember,

$$(\text{Skill} \times \text{Time}) = \text{Value} = \text{Money} = \text{Currency}$$

If one cannot apply their skill because of an accident or sickness, then skill equals zero in the formula, creating zero value. Everyone's most valuable asset at the beginning of this epoch is their ability to create value. This is true regardless of marital or family status.

Probability of Death or Disability before Reaching Full Retirement Age

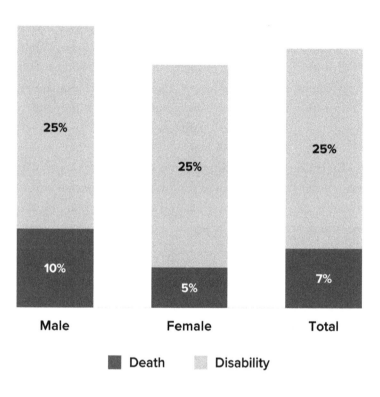

According to the chief actuary of the Social Security Administration (who is wicked smart on this stuff!), about 65 percent of men and 70 percent of women will neither have a disability nor die before age sixty-seven.[68] But that means about 33 percent of us will, and the risk to our wealth is too significant to ignore.

DISABILITY INSURANCE

Handing this risk to an insurance company is a good trade-off for actual danger. Unfortunately, most people's perceived risk tells them this is not a good trade for value.

Mispricing this risk is an example of our cognitive bias driving a decision. Loss aversion (it will not happen to me, and I'll lose the premiums paid) and bad mental accounting (I can afford the loss of income) quickly lead us to poor decisions.

Disability insurance makes sense. You should have enough benefits to pay all your bills for at least five years, and until age sixty-six would be better.

This is true whether you are married or single.

LIFE INSURANCE

Handing this mortality risk to an insurance company is a good trade-off depending on the situation.

Situation One: Single person, no dependents, no one cosigned a loan.

- Simple—Life insurance is not needed as your assets are sold, debts paid, and heirs get what is left over. If you have more debt than assets, the debts die with you.
- The logic is that life insurance is unnecessary if no one depends on your income. (If someone is on the hook as a co-cosigner, then have enough in assets or insurance to pay it off.)

Situation Two: Married/cohabitating, no children.

- Simple—Enough life insurance to pay off all the debts for both plus your annual income for one year.
- The logic here is that the remaining person has lost a partner

emotionally and financially. It seems fair they are moved back to square one financially. Square one is life pre-you, with no debt. Emotionally they should be given the time to grieve without changing their living arrangements, about one year.

- Type of life insurance to buy: Twenty-year level-term insurance. This type of insurance is inexpensive, and the twenty-year term will allow you to accumulate assets over time to protect each other.

Situation Three: Children

- Complicated!—This one's tricky since there are so many variables. Insurance agents and financial planners have formulas to come up with precise numbers.
- A quick hack for the amount is at least ten times your annual gross salary plus all debts the family owes.
- Because of the kids, moving a partner back to a pre-you status is impossible financially. Your lives were built, and a future was planned with a certain amount of income implicit in the bargain.
- Paying off all the debt and providing an income stream from the insurance proceeds means your family can stay in their home; the survivor has time to grieve without financial concerns and can provide for the children's future education.
- Type of life insurance to buy: twenty-year level-term insurance.

---

*The lawyers would want me to remind you, this information is educational and not specific advice. It would be best if you talk to an advisor about your particular situation.

Again, our cognitive biases interfere with this decision-making process. Bad mental accounting, poor perception of risk, and the actual value of future Time all lead to underestimating the genuine risk of early death in a family.

How much should be spent on this program?

Up to 5 percent of your income can be spent on this insurance program to protect the other 95 percent of income for your family.

SELF-INSURANCE

While buying extended warranties makes little sense, losses happen regularly. These are called expected unexpected expenses. Everything wears out eventually.

Sometimes it is a computer monitor, and sometimes it is a job that suddenly ends for reasons beyond our control.

Remember that 10 percent saving hack; these savings should build up cash reserves first.

The amount needed at this stage should be enough to pay your expenses for at least three months and up to one year asking no one for help.

Expenses include:

- Rent or mortgage
- Food
- Utilities
- Transportation
- Property taxes
- Debt payment (minimum payment)

Expenses do not include:

- New clothes
- Vacations
- Nights out

The most significant risk is unexpectedly losing a job. Determine how long it would take to get a new one at the same income to determine the right amount of cash reserves.

Okay, now, the more probable scenario is that we live a long, happy, and successful life.

HACK #3—PROTECT 95 PERCENT WITH 5 PERCENT AND NINETY DAYS OF CASH RESERVES

GOOD THINGS HAPPEN

What constitutes a long, happy, and successful life?

The beauty lies in the fact that everyone gets to define it for themselves. The challenge most face is they never take the time to define what their happy and successful life looks like.

Life often feels like an endless struggle against the ocean currents for these individuals. They constantly battle the surface waves and the undertow below. Unfortunately, some may even get caught in a riptide, being pulled further away from their intended destination.

Our parents and teachers are like lifeguards for the first twenty years of our lives. Their primary role is to keep us safe, protecting us from the riptides of life while also imparting valuable knowledge and skills to help us navigate the currents. Those who make it through this initial stage should thank them for a well-done job.

Our educators, professors, skilled instructors, or managers influence the next phase, lasting around six years in the chosen fields we pursue. They guide us further along our journey, shaping our path and preparing us for what lies ahead.

By age twenty-six, most young adults find themselves removed from their parents' health and car insurance plans. Many rent apartments with friends, secure their first or second jobs, and put into practice the lessons learned from childhood and early adulthood. This is the point in our lives when the real swimming begins.

Most of us stick to the shallows, as serious responsibilities are rarely handed over until we prove our ability to handle them. However, eventually, we all reach the deeper waters of life. The choices we made earlier in building our wealth determine whether we find ourselves in calm, choppy, or dangerous waters.

How we use our future Time becomes crucial in this next epoch of wealth creation. It determines whether safety and success are just a few strong swim strokes away or if we risk being swept out to sea by forces beyond our control.

FAMILY AND FRIENDS

Only a few people have known us our whole lives: mom, dad, brothers, and sisters. They were there before you became the present self you show to the world.

According to psychologists, about half the population rolls into adulthood with secure attachment styles to these folks.[69] In layman's terms, this means you generally enjoy spending time with your aging parents and family. For the other half, family relationships are a challenge fraught with ghosts from the past, which appear at family gatherings. The embarrassing stories, arguments, and grudges begin as soon as the hugs are over.

Over the past thirty years, I've helped guide individuals

through the financial intricacies of family dynamics. It's noteworthy that, despite varying personal feelings, it's usually family members who reach out for help when a parent or sibling needs assistance. This underscores a vital truth: irrespective of past conflicts, fostering and nurturing family relationships is crucial in any effective wealth-building strategy.

Here are some strategies to help maintain and improve these dynamics:

- Open communication—Encourage honest and respectful conversations in which family members can express their feelings, thoughts, and concerns without fear of judgment or criticism.
- Empathy—Cultivate empathy by putting yourself in the other person's shoes and trying to understand their perspective and emotions.
- Apologize and forgive—Be willing to genuinely apologize for any hurt you may have caused and be open to forgiving others for their mistakes.
- Establish boundaries—Set healthy boundaries to ensure each family member feels respected and valued.
- Quality time—Spend time together as a family, engaging in activities everyone enjoys and creating positive memories.
- Establish family rituals and traditions—Create and maintain family rituals and traditions that can help strengthen bonds and create a sense of belonging.
- Self-reflection—Reflect on your behavior, attitudes, and expectations to enhance relationships with family.
- Re-establish trust—Work on rebuilding trust by consistently demonstrating honesty, reliability, and accountability.
- Gratitude and appreciation—Express gratitude and appreciation for each family member, acknowledging their contributions and positive attributes.

For those struggling with these family relationships, reaching out for professional help will make the journey, if not easier, at least more understandable. Resources to help reconnect or improve the family dynamic include resources, such as:

- Professional therapy organizations—Look for organizations like the American Association for Marriage and Family Therapy (AAMFT) or the International Family Therapy Association (IFTA) that provide directories of licensed therapists, educational resources, and information on evidence-based practices.
- Online counseling platforms—Utilize online platforms, such as Talkspace, BetterHelp, or Regain, which offer virtual therapy sessions with licensed therapists, including family therapy.
- Self-help books—Read books on family dynamics, communication, and conflict resolution, such as *The 5 Love Languages* by Gary Chapman; *Difficult Conversations: How to Discuss What Matters Most* by Douglas Stone, Bruce Patton, and Sheila Heen; and *Family Whispering* by Melinda Blau and Tracy Hogg.
- Employee assistance programs (EAPs)—If your employer offers an EAP, take advantage of the resources provided, such as free counseling sessions or referrals to family therapists.

By exploring these resources, you can gain a deeper understanding of family dynamics, improve communication skills, and access professional support to help you and your family navigate challenges and strengthen your relationships.

Learning new tools to deal with these issues will help with the scars from your childhood.

Equally important, it will help prevent scarring the new family you will create and live with through the next two epochs.

FRIENDS, THE FAMILY WE GET TO CHOOSE

Everyone knows the power of friendships. But in building wealth, the presence of close friends helps drive wealth accumulation, and science proves this.

British anthropologist Robin Dunbar developed an insight into relationships that has gained wide acceptance. His contribution was to recognize that the human mind can hold about 150 relationships successfully. His additional contribution was to break this down further to say that these relationships are layered. The layers are five people in the closest layer, ten people in the next layer, thirty-five beyond that, and one hundred people in the final layer.[70] And recent research tells us that focusing on the first two layers leads to better well-being as we grow older.[71]

Indeed, studies from Michigan State University involving nearly 280,000 people found friendships become increasingly important across life's epochs.[72] The studies also found that friendships are stronger predictors of happiness and health in older adults than in family.

The National Institute of Health[73] and others have found the following benefits of having close relationships:

- Increases your sense of belonging and purpose
- Boosts your happiness and reduces your stress
- Improves your self-confidence and self-worth
- Helps you cope with traumas, such as divorce, serious illness, job loss, or the death of a loved one
- Encourages you to change or avoid unhealthy lifestyle habits, such as excessive drinking or lack of exercise

It is clear that having friends is vital to health and happiness. But what does it take to go from acquaintance to close friend?

According to the Journal of Social and Personal Relationships, it takes future Time. A study entitled "How Many Hours Does It Take to Make a Friend?" determined that to move from being an acquaintance to a friend takes about one hundred hours. Becoming a good friend takes two hundred hours, and creating a best friend takes over seven hundred hours.[74]

It is evident that forming friendships requires an investment of Time.

In the postindustrial world controlled by the clock, balancing new relationships with old ones becomes even more critical. Fortunately, existing relationships benefit from Time already invested and need just a bit of watering to maintain their value. While academics study these things, we can probably rely on Mom's advice on maintaining relationships:

- Be kind
- Listen
- Open up
- Be trusted
- Be available

In my experience with close friends, being apart for weeks, months, or even years is irrelevant; we pick up right where we left off. This is true for friends from high school, first jobs, and workout partners from a few years ago.

My experience has taught me that taking the initiative to pick up the phone, send a text, write an email, or note is the crucial first step. So, don't hesitate to reach out and make that call or send that message!

While in-person is best, virtual is a good alternative in a time-starved world. Here are some ways to stay connected:

- Virtual escape rooms—Participate in an online escape room together, solving puzzles and riddles to "escape" within a set time limit. Websites like The Escape Game and Puzzle Break offer virtual escape rooms.
- Online gaming—Play online games together through platforms like Steam, Xbox Game Pass, or PlayStation Now.
- Virtual museum tours—Take virtual tours of famous museums and galleries around the world, such as the Louvre (https://www.louvre.fr/en/visites-en-ligne) or the British Museum (https://www.britishmuseum.org/collection/galleries).
- Virtual reality experiences—Use VR headsets to explore virtual worlds and experiences together. Platforms like AltspaceVR and VRChat offer social VR experiences.
- Watch together—Enjoy movies, TV shows, or videos simultaneously using platforms like Netflix Party, Watch2Gether, or Teleparty.
- Virtual paint nights—Participate in a virtual paint night, in which an instructor guides you through creating a piece of art. Paint With Friends and Yaymaker offer virtual painting events.
- Virtual cooking classes—Attend online cooking classes together and learn new recipes or techniques. Websites like Cozymeal and Sur La Table offer a variety of virtual cooking lessons.
- Virtual wine or beer tastings—Join a virtual wine or beer tasting event to learn about and sample different beverages. Companies like Priority Wine Pass and City Brew Tours offer such experiences.
- Online book clubs—Start a book club with your friend,

discussing books and sharing insights through video calls or online platforms. Websites like BookClubz (https://bookclubz.com/) can help you organize and manage your book club.

- Virtual fitness classes—Take part in online fitness classes or workout challenges using platforms like Peloton or ClassPass.

And while they are in different sections of this book, nothing says your best friend can't be a brother or sister!

All this leads me to say that you should create opportunities for a wide social network. But future Time is typically best spent on the fifteen people in the closest circles.

HACK #4—FAMILY CLOSE, GOOD FRIENDS CLOSER

KNOWLEDGE, EXPERIENCE, WISDOM

As people enter this second epoch of their lives, they have moved beyond the information provided by the textbooks they have read and the tests they have passed. Much of the history, algebra, trigonometry, English, and other minutiae of school have melded along with the real-world needs of incorporating this knowledge into action.

While a writer has little use for the Pythagorean theorem, proper comma placement is critical. Conversely, the comma is of little consequence to a carpenter, but understanding how to calculate the hypotenuse of a triangle means the wall is square. So effectively combining knowledge and experience in the course of the day-to-day is critical to success.

Now, wisdom, that is at a different level. The Wisdom of Solomon is well known. One of my favorite stories is when he is challenged by a group of elders with the question, "What sentence can be used in both good times and bad?"

His answer was "This too shall pass."

While I have not met another Solomon, I have, over my career, met many people from many walks of life. Many had a great deal of formal knowledge and were successful but were always searching for something just beyond their reach.

Others, even those without advanced degrees, internalized life experiences from their craft and relationships and truly understood what they could offer the world. While not always obvious in our first meeting, it became clear over time, based on their questions, decisions, actions, and results that they had acquired wisdom over their lifetime.

What is wisdom?

Wisdom is a deep understanding and realization of concepts, people, and situations based on knowledge, experience, and insight. It is the ability to make sound judgments and decisions by considering various perspectives, consequences, and values. In Part One, I referred to Lincoln's timing and use of the Emancipation Proclamation to help the Union win the Civil War.

This type of wisdom transcends simple intelligence, as it involves knowing facts and how and when to apply that knowledge.

Several key aspects of wisdom include:

- Emotional intelligence—The ability to recognize, understand, and manage our own emotions, as well as empathize with the feelings of others, helps in building wisdom.

- Self-awareness—Knowing our strengths, weaknesses, and biases allows us to make wiser choices and navigate life more effectively.
- Humility—Recognizing we do not know everything and being open to learning from others is essential for developing wisdom.
- Adaptability—Wisdom involves being flexible and accepting change, as well as knowing when to change our perspectives and beliefs.
- Critical thinking—Analyzing information and evaluating its credibility and relevance helps us to refine our understanding and make better decisions.
- Reflection—Regularly reflecting on our experiences, beliefs, and actions allows us to grow and deepen our wisdom.
- Moral compass—Wisdom often involves having a solid ethical foundation that guides our decisions and actions.
- Perspective-taking—Considering different viewpoints and understanding the complexity of situations can lead to more effective problem-solving and decision-making.
- Resilience—Learning from setbacks and using them as opportunities for growth contributes to developing wisdom.
- Compassion—Caring for the well-being of others and working toward the greater good is an essential aspect of wisdom.

One of my favorite couples would disagree with the assessment that they are wise (humility), but they are. Coming from working-class backgrounds, they always had enough but never too much growing up. They carried this perspective into their married life, as they have amassed a small fortune. They never wanted for things and would occasionally splurge, but still, to this day, live well below their means. They ask great questions (critical thinking) and will typically follow suggestions, but not always, if it feels right to them. Being adaptable and frugal, they were able to retire early. They seem genuinely happy together and close to their family (emotional intelligence), looking out for them and each other.

They are individuals who, if dropped into an unusual or unfamiliar social or work situation, would probably manage it successfully using the skills they learned throughout their lives.

Listed below are tools to help you move from simply working from a knowledge base, like a home cook reading a recipe, to applying wisdom to this knowledge to create something special, like a world-class chef:

- Mentorship—Seek the wisdom and guidance of experienced individuals who can provide valuable insights, advice, and feedback to propel your growth.
- Learning from failure—Embrace your mistakes and setbacks as valuable lessons, analyze them to understand what went awry, and use that knowledge to excel in future endeavors.
- Reading—Expand your horizons by delving into diverse subjects and genres, enriching your knowledge base, and exposing yourself to many perspectives.
- Journaling—Regularly capture your thoughts, experiences, and reflections through writing, fostering self-awareness, and nurturing personal development.
- Mindfulness meditation—Cultivate mindfulness to sharpen focus, regulate emotions, and foster a profound understanding of yourself and others.
- Socratic questioning—Challenge your beliefs and assumptions by employing critical self-inquiry, encouraging deep thinking, and fostering comprehensive understanding.

- Active listening—Enhance your communication skills by actively engaging in attentive listening techniques, such as paraphrasing, reflecting, and summarizing others' perspectives.
- Engaging in meaningful conversations—Enrich your understanding by participating in conversations about topics that captivate your interest and spark intellectual growth.
- Practicing empathy—Develop a genuine capacity for empathy, allowing you to truly comprehend the emotions, viewpoints, and experiences of others.
- Cultivating a growth mindset—Foster a mindset that embraces challenges, perseveres through obstacles, and perceives failure as an opportunity for learning and personal development.
- Seeking feedback—Regularly solicit constructive feedback from peers, mentors, or supervisors to identify areas for improvement and fuel continuous growth.
- Lifelong learning—Embrace a commitment to ongoing learning, actively seeking opportunities to acquire new skills, broaden your knowledge, and stay abreast of developments in your field.

The following are things I've learned over the years from experience and other people I hope will help others navigate this epoch:

- Good decisions compound over time, and so do bad ones.
- Long-term goals need long-term plans.
- A good plan executed is better than a perfect one not executed.
- Plan for life in ten, twenty, and thirty years, but live your life now.

- Call your parents—there are not that many calls left.
- Floss.
- Leave open the possibility that you might be wrong.
- Hang around successful people.
- High risk is just high risk; seldom does the return justify it.
- Drugs and alcohol are poison to your life, relationships, and career.
- Treat people as individuals.
- Care less about what other people think.
- Look for mentors, be a mentor.
- The best investment is always in yourself.
- It is okay to say, "I don't know, but I'll find out."
- Live below your means.
- Karma is a real thing; be generous.
- You may not get everything you want, but that's okay.
- Get a good night's sleep.

These one-line thoughts are distilled from Socrates, Jefferson, Gandhi, Naval, and others. The search for wisdom is a journey, not a destination, so I'll close this section with this quote.

"Knowledge can be communicated, but not wisdom. One can find it, live it, be fortified by it, do wonders through it, but one cannot communicate and teach it."

—HERMANN HESSE

HACK #5—HAVE A PLAN TO SEEK EXPERIENCE, KNOWLEDGE, AND WISDOM

JOB, CAREER, CALLING

Let's revisit that study on how people perceive work. That is, people tend to categorize their employment into three distinct mindsets:

- Job—Individuals seeking jobs prioritize a work-life balance, considering work as a means to an end, simply a way to make money.
- Career—Those pursuing careers aspire to climb the ladder, seeking increasing responsibility, promotions, and social recognition as they progress along a defined path.
- Calling—Some individuals view their work as a calling, an integral part of their identity. They find deep personal fulfillment and satisfaction in their jobs, even to the extent that they would continue doing them without compensation.

Surprising to me, the study discovered that approximately equal numbers of individuals within the same profession identified with these three perspectives. It's intriguing that the nature of the job did not significantly impact these orientations. Now, let's briefly reflect on the first epoch of our lives:

- The initial twenty-four years are dedicated to education, encompassing grade school, high school, trade school, apprenticeships, or college.
- Over the next five years, we often navigate various jobs and employers, searching for our footing.

The final stretch of the first epoch revolves around establishing stability, finding a consistent job, nurturing relationships, and building a family. Indeed, the primary objective of the first epoch was to prepare us for the journey ahead.

I have clients in their late twenties and early thirties who are ahead of their peers on the financial curve but still trying to find their place in the world. Few of the younger folks I know or have worked with coming out of the first epoch have discovered their callings or, as others describe it, their passions.

Society is good at telling us what to do, and one of those things is to follow your passion. Unfortunately, it is notoriously bad at telling us how to do it.

What are the ways to move from a job to a passion?

In his TED Talk "How to Live to 100+," Dan Buettner describes the Blue Zones around the world where people live longer than average.[75] In Okinawa, Japan, he uncovered a concept the population embraces called ikigai (pronounced as icky-guy). This can be roughly translated to "a reason for being" or "the reason to wake up in the morning."

Ikigai is the intersection of four essential elements that, when balanced, contribute to a fulfilling and meaningful life:

- Passion—Doing what you love and enjoy allows you to tap into your inner desires, fueling your motivation and enthusiasm.
- Profession—Developing and using your skills and expertise enables you to excel in your chosen field, building confidence and a sense of accomplishment.
- Vocation—Recognizing your role in society and finding ways to contribute positively fosters a sense of responsibility and purpose.
- Mission—Ensuring your passion, skills, and contributions can be financially sustainable helps you achieve economic stability and independence.

Marc Winn converted this to a helpful image in his blog post "What Is Your Ikigai?"[76]

Based on this, it is simple: determine what the world needs and what you are good at that you love to do and that they will pay you for.

This is a great route to find your ikigai.

If you have the Time.

I'll let you in on the secret I've learned from thousands of interviews over thirty years: most people in their fifties and sixties never figured out their calling or ikigai at work. I've often joked with folks that they are still trying to figure out what they want to be when they grow up!

But it is not from lack of trying or desire. It is just that other parts of life became more important, and their passions developed outside of the workplace. The study from earlier that refers to Jobs, Careers, and Callings backs this up, finding that only about one-third of those surveyed felt they had a calling.[77]

And that's okay.

In the TED Talk about ikigai, Buettner expands on this concept by describing a moai in Okinawa. Moais (pronounced mow-eye) are small social groups that provide lifelong companionship. He also provides a clip of a woman with her great-great-granddaughter who says this little girl is her ikigai.

Family and friends are a source of happiness, wealth, and a reason to get up in the morning, go figure!

Perhaps the worst piece of career advice society has embraced is you need to follow your passion to be happy. Why?

- Passion can change over time—What you are passionate about at twenty-six may not be the same as what you are passionate about at forty-six.
- Not everyone has a clear passion—People may have multiple passions that compete with each other.
- Passion may not always pay the bills—Some passions may not have clear career paths or may not pay well. In these cases, blindly following your passion may lead to financial instability and stress.
- Passion can be overrated—While passion is important, it is not the only factor that contributes to success and happiness. Other factors, such as skill, dedication, and a strong work ethic, can also play a significant role.

And passions being overrated is an important consideration. Instead, a calling, or as others describe it, a passion, is developed over time as the knowledge and skills required to excel at the endeavor are mastered and become integral to who we are as people.

Congrats to those born with a unique talent that destines them to find and explore their passion and calling early in life. For the rest of us, there may be some trial and error along the way. For those who are unsure of their purpose, perhaps a better order for finding ikigai is this:

1. First, determine what the world needs.
2. Next, determine who is addressing the world's needs, get hired, and go to work for them and on yourself.
3. Discover what you love to do at this job, and focus on becoming excellent at those things. Take lateral moves, build your skillset, and identify opportunities within and outside your organization. Keep moving to the next opportunity until you accumulate the right combination of skills that you find your ikigai and an organization that allows you to live it.

However, they call it work for a reason. Even the people who have found their calling have things associated with their job they dislike doing. This path requires discipline. As the search for ikigai is a lifelong pursuit, ensuring we stay on the path to discovery is critical.

The following will help, but I must use a phrase and warning my friend Kevin, who has run several businesses, uses after outside consultants offer him plans to upgrade a product or service via a PowerPoint presentation: "Says easy, but does hard."

In his book The Four Agreements, Don Miguel Ruiz offers a framework for staying on the path by proposing four simple yet powerful agreements that individuals can make with themselves.[78] Drawn from the Toltec civilization and philosophy, these teachings emphasize personal freedom and self-awareness. In summary:

- Focus on the power of words and the importance of using them in a truthful and positive manner.
- Work to separate oneself from the opinions and actions of others, promoting a sense of inner peace and emotional detachment.
- Encourage clear communication and understanding to avoid misunderstandings and false beliefs.
- Make a continuous effort toward personal improvement and understand that one's best can vary from moment to moment.

With this framework, we can slowly move to experience flow by building self-confidence and personal growth.

What is flow?

Flow is a psychological state of complete absorption in and focus on an activity, often resulting in a feeling of timelessness and enjoyment. It was first described by psychologist Mihaly Csikszentmihalyi, who found that people who experienced flow reported higher levels of happiness and satisfaction in their lives.[79]

It is crucial to participate in activities that push abilities, but not to the point of causing frustration, to develop a sense of flow. As proficiency grows, so does your level of expertise.

Expertise in a field the world needs is a valuable commodity allowing you to control your future. The process typically takes ten years or more, but once flow is uncovered, so is ikigai.

"Be patient, it takes ten years to build a career in anything."

—@NAVAL

HACK #6—KEEP YOUR AGREEMENTS WITH YOURSELF TO HELP YOU DISCOVER YOUR IKIGAI

THINGS, ALSO CALLED STUFF

In relation to advertising, people never had a chance as they entered this epoch.

Most in their early thirties are looking around at their peers and trying to figure out what is next and what they should be doing. The problem with this is the people they are looking to don't know either, and most are faking it until they make it.

But who is everyone looking to?

The voices from television, social media, radio, and various influencers sway everyone. These media platforms leverage a psychological tactic known as social proof, which banks on people's inclination to mirror others' actions under the assumption those actions are correct. Marketing strategies often feature testimonials, celebrity endorsements, and popular trends to influence consumer behavior. Research suggests that endorsements by celebrities can notably uplift a brand's reputation and prompt consumers to purchase its products.[80]

Media outlets extensively utilize the idea of affective conditioning, which entails creating an association between a product and positive feelings like happiness, love, or accomplishment. Advertisements frequently display attractive individuals, appealing landscapes, and uplifting music to evoke a favorable emotional reaction. This reaction is then linked to the featured product. Studies indicate these positive emotions can significantly impact consumers' attitudes and preferences, consequently shaping their buying decisions.[81]

Another way the media uses psychology is through the

mere exposure effect. This phenomenon occurs when people develop a preference for things they are repeatedly exposed to, as familiarity breeds liking. Advertisers exploit this effect by telling consumers about their products and messages through repeated TV, radio, print, and online advertisements. Studies have found that repeated exposure to ads leads to increased brand awareness and positive attitudes toward products, resulting in higher purchase intentions.[82]

In addition to these psychological principles, the media often targets specific demographics, such as age, gender, or socioeconomic status, to tailor advertising messages and create a sense of personal relevance. For example, toy commercials aimed at children often use bright colors, upbeat music, and the promise of fun and excitement to encourage purchases. Likewise, luxury brands use sophisticated imagery and aspirational messaging to appeal to high-income consumers.

To extrapolate from research, advertisers spend billions of dollars on media campaigns every year. By the time folks reach their early thirties, they will have been exposed to approximately 54,000,000 ads, assuming they encountered 5,000 ads daily for thirty years.[83]

This means, unlike the farmer and baker who exchanged value for value in a fair exchange, we have been manipulated into desiring a lifestyle.

We exchange real value (our Time) for something we've been conditioned to believe is valuable but isn't. This manufactured, influenced lifestyle we exchanged for is fake money.

Seldom does it move us closer to our destination, and many times it slows us down.

People never had a chance.

Until now.

But before we move on, let me confess: I am as susceptible to this as everyone else. I have a nice car, live in a nice house, have nice clothes, and have more grown-up toys than I can play with regularly. I am a perfect example of consumerism, and keeping up with my peers and neighbors has influenced many of my purchases.

But most (not all) came after I had made it. This means putting things in the proper order and prioritizing your needs and wants.

I will not tell anyone what things are important to them. Some things you gotta have. I hope this section provides a framework for you to decipher whether the things on the list are put there by you intentionally or are there unintentionally because of outside influences.

CREATING REFERENCE POINTS FOR THE THINGS IN OUR LIVES

The four agreements listed previously outline a way of thinking that will help counteract the acquisition culture by saying, "Don't take anything personally."

This builds on wisdom from the ancient Greek philosopher Epicurus, who shared:

> Do not spoil what you have by desiring what you have not; remember that what you now have was once among the things you only hoped for.

Hmm, don't take anything personally and be content with what you have; I hear Kevin saying, "Says easy, but does hard."

Okay, we all buy things, some we need and some we want.

To make sure our purchases fit into our lives, we must create a framework for spending. Let's start with a values-based approach.

BUILDING A THING FRAMEWORK

Aligning our purchase decisions to what we have internalized as important to us is critical to making wise purchasing decisions.

A value-sorting exercise can help identify and prioritize your values, guiding your purchasing decisions. Here is a list of values to consider when evaluating potential purchases:

- Financial security
- Health and well-being
- Family and relationships
- Career success
- Education and personal growth
- Environmental sustainability
- Community involvement and social responsibility
- Time management and work-life balance
- Creativity and self-expression
- Spirituality or religious beliefs
- Minimalism and simplicity
- Adventure and exploration
- Cultural appreciation and diversity
- Technological innovation and advancement
- Animal welfare and rights
- Physical fitness and athleticism
- Philanthropy and charitable giving
- Political activism and social justice
- Aesthetic appreciation and beauty
- Tradition and heritage

It is a long list, so eliminate the ones that do not resonate and add any additional values that are important to you. Rank the remaining values in order of importance, with the most critical value at the top of the list.

Once you have your ranked list of values, use it as a reference when evaluating potential purchases. For each big purchase, consider whether it aligns with your values, and prioritize spending on items that support your top values.

But what about those small everyday purchases?

Going through this sorting exercise, some everyday routine purchases begin to fall into place.

- Bring a lunch to work or go out every day?
- Stop for Starbucks or bring a thermos from home?
- Buy the NFL package on cable or basic cable?

Values are strong by this point in our lives, but as we move through this epoch, what we consider to be essential will change. We mature and uncover different talents and interests as we discover our passions and ikigai.

Values are high-level stuff. But let's get in the weeds on the day-to-day stuff; as Ben Franklin puts it, "Beware of little expenses; a small leak will sink a great ship."

While stopping at Starbucks for coffee with a friend or coworker can be an important social event, doing it daily may become the small leak Franklin warns about.

Experience also teaches us the difference between being frugal and being cheap. The difference lies in a person's approach to spending and the prioritization of their values. Frugality is a balanced approach that maximizes value, financial responsibility, and long-term goals. Cheapness is an extreme focus on cost at the expense of quality, relationships, and ethics. Don't be cheap!

"Frugality is the parent of fortune, but cheapness is the enemy of happiness."

—ARTHUR SCHOPENHAUER

TOOLS TO USE ONCE A DECISION IS MADE

If a purchase aligns with our values, how do we decide it is a good purchase decision?

First, remember the Diderot effect.

- Will this purchase require an additional purchase to complete the set?
- If so, what is the total cost of this purchase?

The following techniques are additional tools you can use when making purchases:

- Cost-per-use analysis—Calculate the cost-per-use of an item by dividing its price by the estimated number of times you'll use it. This method can help you determine the actual value of a purchase by considering its long-term utility.
- Opportunity cost assessment—Consider what you're giving up by making a purchase. By evaluating the alternative purchase or savings, you can better determine the relative value of a potential purchase.
- The 10/10/10 Rule—This decision-making technique, proposed by Suzy Welch, asks you to consider how you'll feel about a purchase in ten minutes, ten months, and ten years. This method can help you assess the long-term impact of a purchase on your life and determine whether it's worth the investment.[84]
- The 30-Day Rule—For nonessential purchases, wait thirty

days before making a decision. This technique helps you determine whether the item is essential or just an impulsive desire.

- The Time Rule—Hold a purchase and determine how much of your active Time you need to spend to acquire this product. Assuming you make $100 per day and the item costs $500, would you be willing to spend five days working to acquire this purchase? Your Time is your most valuable asset.

Remember, the media is so effective at selling stuff that Marie Kondo sold seven million copies of a book teaching us how to get rid of stuff we bought that doesn't bring joy!

Outsmart the media and advertisers by aligning your things with your values and finding joy in them. To do this, build your thing framework before you buy.

HACK #7—BUILD A THING/STUFF FRAMEWORK

MONEY—HOW MUCH DO YOU NEED TO BE COMFORTABLE?

As discussed earlier, money is just stored Time. Accumulating money in the postindustrial world ruled by the clock is a math problem with three variables: the amount invested, the Time invested, and growth. Money doubles at a predictable rate according to the Rule of 72.

But as we enter this epoch of our lives, the accumulated lessons we have internalized from our society about money have warped this simple definition of money.

How?

- Our schools emphasize high-paying careers over the personal fulfillment of job satisfaction.
- Our entertainment, like *The Kardashians* and *Real Housewives*, glamorizes the lifestyles of the rich and famous.
- Our social media, TikTok, Instagram, and Facebook influencers all show off their successes, even if they are fake.

And those 54,000,000 ads consumed over the last thirty years have had an impact. This constant barrage of images has led us to believe that extraordinary financial success is necessary for happiness and self-worth.

In the real world, though, studies have suggested that after a certain level of income, happiness and self-worth start to level off. Additionally, there tends to be a weak link between income and happiness overall.[85]

It turns out there is a difference between the means and the measure.

Money can provide access to resources, experiences, and opportunities that enhance our lives. Still, it should not define us as individuals. By focusing on our values, relationships, and personal growth, we can shift our mindsets and develop healthier relationships with money and with others.

We've discovered the challenge to creating monetary wealth is the relationship we have with money. So, how can we develop a positive relationship with money while maintaining healthy connections with others?

- Develop financial self-awareness:
  - Examine your current financial standing, including your income, expenses, debts, savings, and investments.
  - Reflect on your financial beliefs and habits. Consider the factors that have shaped your attitudes toward money,

such as your upbringing, family dynamics, experiences, and cultural background.

Asking the following questions will help you understand this relationship a little better:

- What are my biggest financial fears, and where do they come from?
- How do these fears impact my decision-making and behavior around money?
- What financial aspects frustrate or stress me the most?
- Are there any recurring patterns or habits that contribute to these frustrations?
- How do I envision my ideal financial situation in the future?
- What steps can I take to achieve this vision of financial success and stability?
- How has my upbringing and family background influenced my beliefs and attitudes about money?
- Are there any financial habits or beliefs from my past that I need to reassess or let go of?
- How do my emotions influence my spending, saving, and financial decision-making?
- Do I have any emotional triggers that lead to unhealthy financial behaviors?
- How confident am I in my understanding of personal finance and money management?
- How do my financial beliefs and behaviors impact my relationships with others (e.g., family, friends, romantic partners)?
- What are some specific financial achievements or milestones I am proud of?

This exercise shouldn't take long. It's best if you write down your notes to refer back to later.

The reason to go through this exercise is to think about money and its place in our lives.

Do not shy away from this exercise; it will allow you to better understand past financial decisions and those you will make in the future.

Few of the thousands of people I have met over the years understand this relationship.

I know this because at the beginning of every planning relationship, I ask a simple question, "How much income do you need to be comfortable?"

Typically, I'm met with silence and a bewildered stare. If I meet with a couple, they might nervously look at each other and shrug. Inevitably, the answer is, "Gosh, I don't know."

Early in my career, I found this surprising. How could you not know?

It seemed so obvious to me. But as time passed, it finally dawned on me why this was the case for most people. I came to understand that when income is an objective term ($50,000, $75,000, $100,000), it is easy to throw out a number.

The hard part of the question is defining "comfortable."

Comfortable is a subjective concept that few have even considered. Comfort has its roots in the past, which directs future decisions. Understanding where money fits into your life allows you to understand what comfort level is required to be satisfied.

Broadly, comfort has several dimensions:

- Physical—This refers to a state of physical well-being in which an individual is free from pain or discomfort and can meet basic physical needs, such as food, shelter, and clothing.
- Environmental—This refers to comforts in one's physical

environment, such as having a comfortable living space, access to nature, and a sense of safety and security.

- Emotional—This refers to a state of emotional well-being, in which an individual feels at ease and content with their life circumstances. Emotional comfort can involve feeling secure in one's relationships, having a sense of purpose, and feeling fulfilled in one's daily activities.
- Financial—This refers to a state of financial stability in which an individual can meet their basic needs and some of their wants without feeling stressed or anxious about money.

We can classify these four basic requirements as an acceptable level of comfort.

Most have this level of comfort by the time Epoch II has begun. Our jobs cover rent in an area in which we feel comfortable. We can afford to get together with family and friends for gatherings and nights out, and most of us can set a little money aside for emergencies.

The next level is an aspirational level of comfort, which might include:

- Owning a home in a desirable neighborhood or city that meets specific needs and preferences.
- Boosting income through career growth, further education, training, or launching a side business.
- Saving for long-term financial goals, such as retirement, a down payment on a home, or a child's education.
- Planning trips for exploring new destinations or indulging in luxurious experiences like international travel or luxury accommodations.

But these could be considered traditional comforts. Some folks have a different view of comfort:

- Professional hobo—Nora Dunn has been a digital nomad since 2006. Her blog, theprofessionalhobo.com, describes her as an expert on long-term travel, personal finance, remote work, and lifestyle design.
- Homesteader—Helen and Scott Nearing were a couple who lived a self-sufficient lifestyle on a homestead in Vermont for over sixty years. They built their home, grew their own food, and generated their own electrical power.
- Family of sailors—Samantha Kalil and her husband Aaron purchased a forty-two-foot sailboat and took off to travel and homeschool their children.

As stated, comfort is subjective once you take care of the basics. While the previous exercise of looking back at what has transpired to impact feelings about money should only take an hour, defining comfort will be an ongoing exercise as it changes over time.

The following questions help quantify this concept of comfort better, both at the beginning of this epoch and as it goes on.

- Housing
    - How satisfied am I with my current housing situation?
    - What aspects of my living space do I appreciate, and which areas could be improved?
    - How important are factors like storage, outdoor space, and soundproofing to my overall satisfaction with my living environment?
    - How does my housing location affect my daily life and access to transportation?

- In what ways does my living space provide a sense of privacy and security?
- How can I adjust the temperature and lighting in my living space to maximize comfort?

- Financial
  - How confident am I in my current emergency fund, and does it cover three to six months of living expenses?
  - Do I have adequate life, health, home, and auto insurance coverage?
  - How diversified is my investment portfolio, and am I satisfied with its growth potential?
  - What is my plan for paying off debt and reducing financial stress?
  - How often do I utilize financial planning resources, such as financial advisors or online tools?
  - How am I saving for significant life events like buying a home or starting a family?
  - What is my approach to charitable giving or supporting causes I care about?

- Health and Wellness
  - How do I regularly engage in self-care practices like meditation or yoga?
  - How do my relationships with friends and family provide emotional support?
  - How am I managing any chronic health conditions or disabilities?
  - How accessible are healthy food options and clean drinking water in my daily life?
  - Do I have a safe and comfortable environment for exercise, such as a gym or fitness studio?
  - How often do I use outdoor recreation opportunities like parks or trails?

- Career and Education
  - What is my plan for continuing education or professional development in my field?
  - Have I sought out opportunities for mentorship or coaching in my career?
  - How fulfilled and satisfied am I with my current work situation?
  - Are flexible work arrangements (remote work or flexible schedules) available to me, and how do they impact my work-life balance?
  - How well does my career align with my values and provide a sense of purpose?
  - What steps am I taking to maintain a healthy work-life balance?
- Relationships and Community
  - How often do I engage in social activities and connect with like-minded individuals?
  - How would I rate the quality of my relationships with family and friends?
  - How frequently do I participate in cultural or community events that align with my interests and values?
  - In what ways do I volunteer or contribute to my community?
  - How strong is my sense of belonging and connection to a community or group?
  - How willing am I to seek new social connections and expand my network?
- Overall Well-Being
  - What opportunities do I have for creative expression, such as writing or art?
  - How often do I utilize resources for personal growth and development?

- How satisfied am I with my personal and professional accomplishments and fulfillment?
- How do I prioritize relaxation and leisure activities, such as travel or hobbies?
- How connected do I feel to something larger than myself, like spirituality or nature?
- What steps can I take to seek support and resources to improve my overall well-being?

As you examine your world, do as Margery Leveen Sher suggests in her book, *The Noticer's Guide to Living and Laughing*, and be a "noticer."[86] Be present and take note of what is going right and wrong in your life to improve the situation.

Once your comfort level has been identified, written down, talked about, and agreed to, you can accumulate enough to acquire those things you need and want. At this point, accumulating it is easy once you separate money from self-worth and internalize that money is a means to allow you to lead a comfortable life. Well, okay, not easy, but easier!

"Thinking about the future will cause it to change."

—THOMAS FREY

HACK #8—ACCUMULATE TO BE COMFORTABLE AND UNDERSTAND YOUR COMFORTABLE

STRATEGY TO ACCUMULATE $1,000,000
IN MONETARY WEALTH

The Barenaked Ladies had a hit song in the 1990s called "If I Had $1,000,000." It was a fun, catchy tune. Most everyone is familiar with the international game show sensation, *Who Wants to Be a Millionaire?* And, when I ask, prospective clients will often say, "I think a million dollars would be enough."

This million-dollar figure is firmly engraved on our collective consciousness as an almost unattainable amount of money. It's an amount so large it would be enough to solve our financial problems and set us up for life.

While in reality this is just a random number, many people aspire to achieve a net worth of $1,000,000. It's a common goal and one that presents a significant challenge.

In fact, out of the estimated 217 million people in the United States over the age of twenty-five, only 22 million have achieved this milestone. A select few are born into wealth, but they are the minority as there are only about 100,000 multimillionaires in the United States.[87]

Some lucky individuals stumble into wealth through extraordinary, non-replicable events like winning a lottery or a trifecta at the track but most of us embark on a daily work journey to make ends meet.

This routine might seem mundane until you realize this endeavor is more than work. It's carving out a career, finding your ikigai, providing for a family, and providing the tools for amassing the financial means to attain a desired comfort level.

It will take most of us a while to accumulate $1,000,000. How much time depends a lot on strategy and a little on luck.

Let's review these two factors, and to do this, let me bring back our fictional character, Matrix, and fill you in on his imaginary backstory. We will start with strategy.

From a young age, Matrix shows a natural talent for art and feels a strong connection to the creative process. Recognizing the traditional college route was not the right fit, Matrix dedicates himself to a life of pursuing art as a career. At thirty-three, Matrix finds the perfect job creating art. The job pays him $35,000 per year. After years of sleeping on friends' couches, Matrix considers this a great gig.

In this fulfilling role, Matrix focuses on creating art and is content with the income it generates. Unknowingly, Matrix has discovered ikigai, the perfect blend of passion, profession, vocation, and mission!

Over the years, Matrix turned down opportunities for promotions and increased earnings because true happiness for Matrix was in his artistic pursuit. Fortunately, Matrix received pay raises of 3 percent per year. This allowed Matrix to continue living a meaningful life, deeply immersed in art, while maintaining financial stability for the thirty-three years of Epoch II.

Matrix knew this job would end at some point, so he employed a simple strategy of saving for the future.

Matrix saved $1,750 per year (5 percent of his $35,000 income) plus 33 percent of any pay above the starting pay of $35,000, assuming a 10.32 percent annual return. That looks like this:

Year	Matrix's Income with 3% Pay Raises	Matrix Spends Each Year	Matrix's Base Savings	33% of Amount over $35,000	Matrix Saves Each Year	Matrix's Savings-Account Growth
1	35,000	33,250	1,750	0	1,750	1,750
2	36,050	33,954	1,750	347	2,097	4,027
3	37,132	34,678	1,750	703	2,453	6,896
4	38,245	35,424	1,750	1,071	2,821	10,429
5	39,393	36,193	1,750	1,450	3,200	14,705
6	40,575	36,985	1,750	1,840	3,590	19,812
7	41,792	37,801	1,750	2,241	3,991	25,848
8	43,046	38,641	1,750	2,655	4,405	32,920
9	44,337	39,506	1,750	3,081	4,831	41,149
10	45,667	40,397	1,750	3,520	5,270	50,665
11	47,037	41,315	1,750	3,972	5,722	61,616
12	48,448	42,260	1,750	4,438	6,188	74,163
13	49,902	43,234	1,750	4,918	6,668	88,484
14	51,399	44,237	1,750	5,412	7,162	104,777
15	52,941	45,270	1,750	5,920	7,670	123,261
16	54,529	46,334	1,750	6,445	8,195	144,176
17	56,165	47,430	1,750	6,984	8,734	167,789
18	57,850	48,559	1,750	7,540	9,290	194,395
19	59,585	49,722	1,750	8,113	9,863	224,320
20	61,373	50,920	1,750	8,703	10,453	257,923
21	63,214	52,153	1,750	9,311	11,061	295,601
22	65,110	53,424	1,750	9,936	11,686	337,793
23	67,064	54,733	1,750	10,581	12,331	384,985
24	69,076	56,081	1,750	11,245	12,995	437,710
25	71,148	57,469	1,750	11,929	13,679	496,561
26	73,282	58,899	1,750	12,633	14,383	562,189
27	75,481	60,372	1,750	13,359	15,109	635,315
28	77,745	61,889	1,750	14,106	15,856	716,736
29	80,077	63,452	1,750	14,876	16,626	807,328
30	82,480	65,061	1,750	15,668	17,418	908,063
31	84,954	66,719	1,750	16,485	18,235	1,020,010
32	87,503	68,427	1,750	17,326	19,076	1,144,351
33	90,128	70,186	1,750	18,192	19,942	1,282,390

This means Matrix maintains a reasonable living standard but increases his standard of savings over the years.

Now for the luck part. Please stick with me on this; it gets a little tricky.

In finance, we use a tool called Monte Carlo simulation to make educated guesses of the potential outcomes of investing. Picture it like a game of roulette at the famous Monte Carlo casino in Monaco, from where this simulation gets its name. In roulette, there is an uncertain outcome with every spin of the wheel. The same is true for an investment portfolio where good or bad news, like the croupier casting the marble, changes the outcome every minute of every day, month, year, and decades.

In our example, Matrix invested in the stock market for thirty-three years, and there are three possible results:

- A best-case scenario where the market could boom.
- A likely scenario where the market performs about average; this is the Matrix-savings scenario used above.
- A worst-case scenario where the market could crash.

Using a Monte Carlo simulation, we run thousands of scenarios using different combinations of factors, such as market trends, economic indicators, and past performance. It's like viewing thousands of potential future realities where the three possible scenarios all come into sharper focus.

Matrix's Monte Carlo simulation was executed 10,000 times, and the results were:

- Best case, Matrix ends up with about $3 million.
- The likely, shown in the table, Matrix ends with about $1.3 million, crossing the million-dollar threshold between years

twenty-eight and thirty-five. Note that 10.32 percent was the estimated return used in the Matrix-savings scenario.
• The worst case, Matrix has about $610,000 at thirty-three years. It takes five more years to hit $1,000,000.

Monte Carlo, while just sophisticated guessing, offers a glimpse of the possible future results for Matrix.

The likelihood is that Matrix, in our example, will end up with somewhere between $1 million and $2 million, possibly a little more, perhaps a little less. The same is true for anyone who follows a strategy of saving consistently over time.

Here are some examples:

• Ronald Read was a gas station attendant and janitor from Brattleboro, Vermont. Throughout his lifetime, he saved and invested more than $8 million by living frugally and making wise stock investments. When he passed away in 2014 at ninety-two, he left most of his fortune to the local hospital and library.[88]
• Grace Groner worked as a secretary for Abbott Laboratories in Illinois. In 1935, she purchased three shares of Abbott stock for $180. Over the years, her investment grew through dividend reinvestment and stock splits. When she passed away in 2010 at one hundred, her Abbott shares were worth approximately $7 million. She left her fortune to her alma mater, Lake Forest College, to establish a scholarship fund.[89]

There are many more stories, but they all sum up the same: a person who never made much money lived frugally and saved consistently.

They then put their money in the way of things that would grow.

Not to diminish their investment acumen, but Charlie Munger and Warren Buffet have another secret to their impressive wealth accumulation. Munger died at age ninety-nine, and Buffett is ninety-three. They both have had one more doubling in their lifetimes than most people. And as we know from our water lily farmer, it is the last doubling that is the most important.

Remember, monetary wealth is a math problem with three variables,

1. Amount
2. Time
3. Growth

Matrix was given two of these: time and amount. How was growth determined?

Let's refer to the farmer, baker, and blacksmith. If you recall, a bond means lending someone money with the promise you will be repaid. A stock is an investment in a business as an owner.

Like Matrix, an investor who understands Time and the Rule of 72 understands the need to earn higher returns to get one more doubling during their Accumulation Epoch, and stocks are the answer. Bonds are the answer for someone who already has accumulated enough assets and does not need to double their assets to be successful.

In all the Monte Carlo scenarios, Matrix chose a 100 percent stock portfolio.

According to the Monte Carlo analysis, the rate of return ranged from about 6 percent for the no-luck Matrix to about 14 percent for the very lucky Matrix over the thirty-three years of Epoch II. The worst year for the no-luck Matrix was –61 percent, while the very lucky Matrix's worst year was –32 percent.

In another scenario, Matrix decided instead to invest in 100 percent bonds, which are generally considered less risky.

According to the Monte Carlo analysis, the rate of return ranged from 3.95 percent for the no-luck Matrix to 6.26 percent for the very lucky Matrix over the thirty-three years of this epoch. The worst year for the no-luck Matrix was –19 percent, while the very lucky Matrix's worst year was –5.86 percent.

If Matrix is overly cautious, none of the scenarios cross $1,000,000 by age sixty-six.

Growth, by nature, possesses an element of unpredictability and a touch of luck. However, it is through growth that most individuals have the opportunity to generate substantial financial wealth over time.

While we can guess at the future, we can analyze the past. In a real-world comparison of portfolios, we can see the historical impact of where different decisions might have led us.

Comparison of Various Portfolios 1994–2023

	0% / 100%	20% / 80%	40% / 60%	60% / 40%	80% / 20%	100% / 0%
Equity	0%	20%	40%	60%	80%	100%
Fixed Income	100%	80%	60%	40%	20%	0%
Annualized Return (1/1/94–12/31/23)	4.24%	5.63%	6.90%	8.05%	9.06%	9.92%
Worst Calendar Year % (Year)	-13.25% / 2022	-14.52% / 2022	-15.79% / 2022	-20.20% / 2008	-28.62% / 2008	-37.04% / 2008
Best Calendar Year % (Year)	18.18% / 1995	21.70% / 1995	25.22% / 1995	28.74% / 1995	32.26% / 1995	35.79% / 1995
Rule of 72 — Approximate Number of Doublings	1.8	2.3	2.9	3.4	3.8	4.1
Estimated Growth $1,000 (1/1/94–12/31/23)	3,479	5,178	7,411	10,199	13,481	17,079

Now, let's return to our strategic perspective. Matrix had a long-term savings plan, intending to invest his money for thirty-three years until the age of sixty-six—marking the end of this epoch. This strategy was chosen because the potential upside return justifies the inherent downside risk.

However, it's important to note that if Matrix requires funds in the short term—for purposes like purchasing a car, going on vacation, or making a down payment on a new home—then it is advisable to place that money in a relatively safe and easily accessible asset, such as short-term bonds or cash. This cautious approach is warranted because the potential downside risk outweighs the expected upside return in such a short time frame.

By carefully aligning investment strategies with specific time horizons and weighing the potential risks and rewards, individuals like Matrix can navigate the financial landscape more effectively, leveraging growth for long-term wealth accumulation while protecting their shorter-term financial needs.

"The best way to measure your investing success is not by whether you're beating the market but by whether you've put in place a financial plan and a behavioral discipline that are likely to get you where you want to go."

—Benjamin Graham

*The lawyers would want me to remind you that no one can predict the future and that past performance is not a guarantee of future results! This is not investment advice. It is just educational in nature. The data is derived from Portfolio Visualizer 1/1/1994–12/31/2023.

HACK #9—PUT YOUR ASSETS IN THE WAY OF THINGS THAT GENERATE REAL RETURNS

TIME

Earlier, we touched on how we perceive time as we grow older and how most of the population interacts with time. We have moved from the agrarian society of our ancestors working the land to one that involves highly specialized skills.

This change means our skills are measured in minutes, not seasons, and on the whole, we are compensated as such. Hourly workers are directly paid for their Time. They can quickly answer how much they earn.

Salaried workers are paid for their skills but are still expected to put in a full-time effort of 2,000+ hours a year. Over the years, most divide their annual salary by 2,000 hours to calculate an hourly rate (I know I have!).

Whether we are paid hourly or by salary, everyone in this postindustrial world ruled by the clock has looked up at that clock on the wall and wondered when the day would be over. While it may seem we have unlimited amounts, Time is slipping away.

As we enter and move through Epoch II of life, Time becomes the most critical variable. It impacts relationships, careers, and financial security. How we take advantage of it is essential. But it is tough to visualize the future from where we stand.

The following is adapted from the website *Wait But Why*,[90] which breaks a human life down into months. I've refined this a bit and broken the months into the three thirty-three-year epochs we live through.

Year	Epoch I	Epoch II	Epoch III
1			
2			
3			
4			
5			
6			
7			
8			
9			
10			
11			
12			
13			
14			
15			
16			
17			
18			
19			
20			
21			
22			
23			
24			
25			
26			
27			
28			
29			
30			
31			
32			
33			

This means there are 1,188 months in a lifetime, and each epoch equals 396 months.

Year	Epoch I	Epoch II	Epoch III
1			
2			
3			
4			
5			
6			
7			
8			
9			
10			
11			
12			
13			
14			
15			
16			
17			
18			
19			
20			
21			
22			
23			
24			
25			
26			
27			
28			
29			
30			
31			
32			
33			

According to Dalbar Inc., equity investors have averaged a 6.81 percent yearly return since 1993.[91] According to the Rule of 72, 72 divided by 6.81 = 10.57 years. Using this, I've broken the epochs into eleven-year doubling blocks.

Now the luckiest among us might get ten doublings (think Munger and Buffett), and the least lucky seven or eight doublings in a lifetime.

SAVING AND INVESTING

Focusing on the nine likely doublings in our lifetime, it becomes clear the first two are periods when we have no ability to save any money. We are just learning how to survive. The last three are probably a time when we draw from the assets we've accumulated to support our lives after we stop working.

This means most of us have four doubling blocks to grow our wealth to support our lifestyles once we stop saving.

If one understands the Rule of 72, it becomes clear how someone who is a consistent saver from age eighteen can accumulate $1,000,000 faster than someone who starts with a higher income at age thirty-three.

The younger saver has one more doubling of their savings than those starting in their late twenties to early thirties. The mathematics of compounding means the value invested grows well after two doublings but takes off after the third doubling.

The Matrix saving example outlined previously is one method; there are additional strategies in the Savings Appendix.

Regardless, all we can do as investors is put our money in the way of things that can earn us consistently higher returns than leaving cash in a savings account.

HACK #10—USE TIME AND THE RULE OF 72 TO YOUR ADVANTAGE

RELATIONSHIPS

While less mathematical than investing money, visualize ways to compound your meaningful relationships over a lifetime using the same nine doubling boxes.

Like money, the first two doubling boxes are a period of learning about relationships and surviving. We all experience the heartbreak of first loves, broken and lost friendships, and discovering ourselves and what is essential in a partner.

The third doubling box for many is looking for a stable relationship to enter our next life phase. Studies have indicated there are many factors involved, but here are a few examples that lead to a successful relationship:

- Shared values—Research has consistently found that shared values and beliefs are important for the success of a romantic relationship. Understanding your potential partner's values is fundamental.[92]
- Emotional maturity—Research has shown that emotional intelligence is a significant predictor of relationship satisfaction and success.[93]
- Compatibility—Research has suggested that having similar personality traits can be important for relationship satisfaction.[94]
- Respect and kindness—Research has consistently found that respect, kindness, and empathy are important for healthy relationships.[95]

According to the US Census, the median age of first marriage is about thirty for men and twenty-eight for women, leading us into the next epoch.[96] Like money, investing small but consistent deposits into a relationship allows for compounding over time. Examples of this include:

- Saying "thank you" often—Expressing gratitude for your partner's actions, even for small things, can show appreciation and strengthen the relationship.
- Complimenting your partner—Let your partner know what you admire about them and what qualities you appreciate.
- Writing a love note—Leave a sweet message for your partner expressing how much you love and appreciate them.
- Doing something unique—Surprise your partner with a thoughtful gesture, such as preparing their favorite meal or planning a special outing.

- Listening attentively—Give your partner your undivided attention when they are speaking and show that you value their thoughts and feelings.
- Showing physical affection—A simple hug, kiss, or touch is a powerful way to show your love and appreciation for your partner.
- Celebrating milestones—Whether it's a birthday, anniversary, or other special occasion, take the time to celebrate with your partner and show them how much you care.

In our busy lives, it's essential to create a process to remember to show gratitude and appreciation in our relationships. Without a plan, your career, kids, and other important responsibilities can take over and leave little room for building meaningful connections. Therefore, it's crucial to create a system to stay on track. Here are several ideas to get started:

- Use a calendar app or reminder system to schedule regular reminders to express gratitude and appreciation to your partner. For example, you could schedule a reminder every Friday to write a love note or plan a special date night. You can also set reminders to express gratitude in small ways throughout the day, such as texting or saying "thank you" for a kind gesture.
- Set up a jar or box in your home for which you and your partner can write things you're grateful for about each other. Take turns reading the notes out loud to each other and celebrating the things you appreciate. This can be a fun and interactive way to build gratitude and appreciation in your relationship.
- Use your calendar to plan special dates and outings with your partner, such as a weekend getaway or a romantic dinner.

These can be great opportunities to express gratitude and appreciation in a fun and memorable way. Schedule these dates and stick to them to ensure they happen regularly.

- Keep a gratitude journal and write something you're grateful for about your partner daily. You can share these notes with your partner to express appreciation and strengthen your connection.
- Set aside regular time to discuss your relationship with your partner. This can be an excellent opportunity to express gratitude and appreciation and discuss any concerns or challenges. You can schedule these check-ins on your calendar. Remember, like with savings, small, consistent actions can have a big impact on building a strong and meaningful relationship. By creating a system to remind yourself to show gratitude and appreciation, you can compound your relationship over time and create a fulfilling and satisfying connection.

HACK #11—RELATIONSHIPS COMPOUND; INVEST IN THEM REGULARLY

CALLING

Some people seem destined for greatness and, luckily, discover their calling early in life.

- Mozart was composing music at five years old.
- Picasso was producing artwork in his teens.
- Elon Musk sold his first video game at age twelve and co-founded a web software company at age twenty-four.

However, most of us search for our true purpose as we move into the next chapter of our lives. For those individuals, it's crucial to actively engage with their work to inch closer to their ikigai. Here are a few strategies to help transform your current job into a more meaningful and fulfilling experience:

- Recognize your impact—Understand how your work contributes to your organization's larger goals and makes a difference in people's lives. Reflect on the positive outcomes and value created by your tasks.
- Align with your values—Identify your core values and find ways to integrate them into your work. This will help you find a sense of purpose and increase job satisfaction.
- Build positive relationships—Cultivate strong connections with colleagues, supervisors, and clients. Supportive and meaningful workplace relationships can make your job more enjoyable and help you feel more connected to your work.
- Seek growth opportunities—Expand your skills and knowledge in your current role. This could involve volunteering for new projects, taking on additional responsibilities, or pursuing training and development opportunities.
- Set personal goals—Establish clear objectives and milestones in your current job that align with your long-term career goals and aspirations. This will keep you motivated and focused on growth and progress.
- Find your flow—Identify tasks and activities that engage you and allow you to enter a state of flow, where you're fully absorbed and enjoy what you're doing. Try to include these activities in your work routine.
- Develop a growth mindset—Embrace challenges and see setbacks as opportunities for growth and learning. This

mindset will help you become more resilient and adaptable, making your job more rewarding.

- Maintain work-life balance—Prioritize self-care and balance your personal and professional lives. This balance will help you feel more fulfilled and prevent burnout.
- Practice gratitude—Regularly reflect on the aspects of your job that you enjoy or appreciate. Acknowledging the positive aspects of your work can help shift your perspective and cultivate a sense of fulfillment.
- Take charge—If there are certain aspects of your job that make it hard for you to feel fulfilled and satisfied, think about having a conversation with your supervisor to address these concerns. Together, you can brainstorm solutions or potential adjustments to your role that better align with your calling.

By focusing on these areas, you'll build a firm foundation for future wealth and satisfaction in life.

As we approach the next epoch, what does our Time balance sheet look like?

Wealth Era — End of Epoch II

Account	Asset	Liability
Parents	5	5
Siblings	33	17
Friends	33	17
Children	14	14
Mentorships	10	0
Experiences	66	0
Knowledge	50	0
Wisdom	20	0
Things/Stuff	20	5
Financial Assets	33	0
Time	<u>33</u>	<u>0</u>
Total	317	58
Net Worth		**259**

The sands of the hourglass continue to fall, and we have depleted 66 percent of our allotted Time. The same goes for our support network; we are all getting older.

We have picked up a new asset, children. They are probably neither a help nor a hindrance. They are in their thirties, starting families of their own, and while they may look to us for some babysitting, they are not a significant financial burden. We might still have a parent alive; if so, they are leaning on us for more and more.

Our liabilities are shrinking. We've paid off the loans on most of our stuff, and our education loans are long gone, though we still have some of the kids' education costs we handle over the next few years.

"Beautiful young people are accidents of nature, but beautiful old people are works of art."

—ELEANOR ROOSEVELT

TAKEAWAYS

Keep in mind your goal—to build wealth. As we find ourselves in life's middle stage, time can feel like it's speeding up, responsibilities mount, and while some dreams become a reality, others may need to be set aside temporarily. Rest assured; you'll navigate this phase successfully.

Charting a course for the future is crucial, and your wealth foundation will be the collective result of:

- Reliable relationships—Your network of family and friends offering love, support, and companionship.
- Learned lessons and wisdom—The invaluable life teachings, insights, and knowledge you've amassed over time.
- Job satisfaction and worth—Your connection to your work, finding contentment and purpose in your career.
- Beloved possessions—The things you keep around you that provide joy, comfort, and usefulness.

- Built-up financial resources—The money you've diligently saved and invested for a secure financial future.
- Efficient Time management—Your skill in balancing Time for responsibilities, relationships, personal growth, and leisure.

Pour resources into yourself, the people you care about, your work, and your future.

Small, consistent improvements across all facets of your life can compound over time, working in your favor. Occasionally, some parts of your life may demand more Time than others. Be mindful of this and strive to replenish the Time balance in other areas when available.

This phase of safeguarding and accumulating sets the stage for your next epoch—the time for drawing on or passing on your wealth.

CHAPTER 9

EPOCH III: WITHDRAWING/ PASSING TIME—AGE SIXTY-SIX TO AGE NINETY-NINE

The journey of self-discovery and living our ikigai continues and takes on a deeper meaning at this stage of our lives. Time, the most precious and nonrenewable resource, steadily depletes as we age, yet the beauty of life lies in the richness we accumulate in other aspects. Family, friends, experiences, knowledge, wisdom, possessions, and money are the pillars that shape our existence and define our true wealth.

The Wealth Equation from earlier in the book makes more sense at this point in our lives.

$$Wealth = FF + EKW + J + S + FA + T$$

(Family, Friends, Experience, Knowledge, Wisdom, Job, Stuff, Financial Assets, Time)

This next epoch of our lives is both the most fun and the least certain.

It is the least certain because, although we refrain from discussing the topic, we understand that Time is running out. As mentioned at the outset, we are all given the gift of Time; we just don't know how much. But it is probably more than you think.

As I tell my clients, their best case is a long, healthy life, which is also the hardest to plan. Making sure resources outlast us for thirty years requires a lot of thought.

This is why I use age ninety-nine as the end of this epoch. While today relatively few people make it to this ripe old age, looking forward, quite a few of us will.

LIFE SPAN

The first data point to consider is life expectancy. The Social Security Administration has a good handle on how long people will live since they must send monthly checks to retirees.

Period Life Table, 2020, as Used in the 2023 Trustees Report

	Male		Female	
Exact Age	Number of Lives	Life Expectancy	Number of Lives	Life Expectancy
0	100,000	74	100,000	80
33	96,308	43	98,171	48
66	74,986	16	85,063	19
74	60,827	11	74,479	13
80	45,397	7	60,931	9
84	33,015	6	48,372	7
99	861	2	2,657	2

They publish mortality tables that look at the population from birth to age 119.[97] Markers at the beginning and end of each epoch look like this:

At birth (exact age, zero), of the 100,000 males born, the average man is expected to live (life expectancy) to age seventy-four. But if he reaches age seventy-four, he is expected to live another eleven years. Women at birth are expected to live until age eighty. But if they make it, they are expected to live another nine years.

Moreover, the longer a person lives, the longer they are

expected to live. It makes sense. If we avoided the things that killed the other folks in our age cohort, our genes or common-sense avoidance of risk means we are being selected to live longer.

Based on this chart, around 75 percent of individuals entering this era survive for ten years, 35 percent survive for twenty years, and only 1 percent reach the age of ninety-nine.

But this chart is based on history. And history looked something like this in 1950:

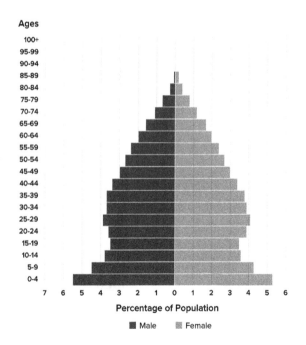

U.S. Population Estimates — 1950

The axis on the left shows age groups in five-year increments, such as age zero to four or fifteen to nineteen. The bottom axis shows the percentage of the population in each age group with the percentages on the left being male and those on the right female. The population of the United States was about 148 million people.

This graph shows the impact of the baby boom generation (age zero to four) and the impact of two World Wars that affected those between fifteen to nineteen and twenty to twenty-four years old. The graph shows a pyramid shape, with fewer and fewer people as we move up the age groups and very few people in their eighties and nineties. This fat at the bottom and skinny at the top pattern has been the norm throughout history.

U.S. Population Estimates — 2050

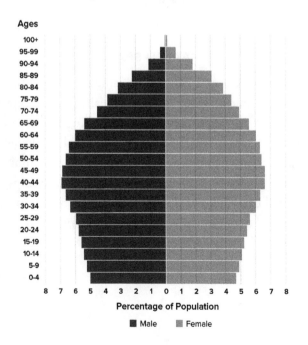

But fast forward one hundred years to 2050, and that graph is expected to look like this:

In the 1950 graph, about one percent of the population reached their eighties and beyond. But by the 2050 projection, that number has increased to about ten percent. The future looks to be more of a tunnel than a pyramid.[98]

The population has grown to be 360 million people, meaning, not only are people expected to live longer, but we also have more people living longer lives.

And this projection is before the impact of a tremendous number of medical and technological advances being worked on increasing life expectancy. According to the *Wall Street Journal*, geroscientists (an entirely new field of study) are undertaking research that might extend life expectancy to age 125.[99]

This change affects how we think through Time, for both ourselves and those we care about.

HEALTH SPAN

While life expectancy is witnessing astounding growth, granting us more time on this journey, our health has not kept up.

The more accurate measure of a fulfilling life lies in the quality of those years in addition to the number. The notion of health span encompasses our physical and mental well-being, our ability to engage in meaningful relationships, and our overall enjoyment of life. By focusing on health span, we can ensure that our extended years are filled with vibrancy and fulfillment.[100]

Life Span versus Health Span

% of our Time
spent with illness

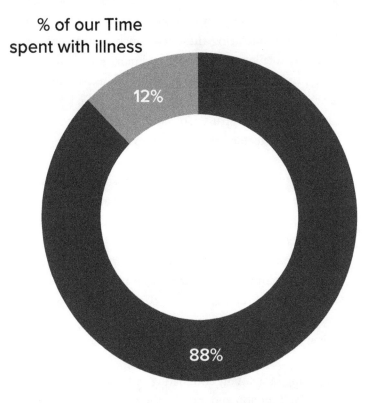

12%

88%

% of our Time spent healthy

Life span is the total number of years lived by an individual. Health span is the number of disease-free years lived. Life and health-adjusted life expectancy are population-level measures of life span and health span, respectively. A gap of nine years is deducted from comparing 2020 data for a median probabilistic projection of life expectancy and health-adjusted life expectancy.

Our relationships with family and friends powerfully shape our health spans. Studies consistently demonstrate the profound impact of social connections on our well-being.[101] Strong bonds with loved ones provide emotional support, reduce stress levels, and even bolster our immune systems. Investing Time and effort into nurturing these relationships can contribute significantly to a longer, healthier, and more joyful life.

As we navigate the aging journey, we appreciate time's preciousness. Effectively utilizing our Time can have a profound impact on our health spans. Consider the following stats.

Engaging in regular physical activity:

- Regular physical activity has been consistently shown to improve overall health and increase longevity.
- Embrace an active lifestyle, no matter your age, and enjoy its numerous benefits.
- Incorporate activities like walking, swimming, yoga, or strength training into your routine to promote physical fitness and well-being.[102]

Pursuing mentally stimulating activities:

- Engaging in mentally stimulating activities helps maintain cognitive function and reduces the risk of age-related cognitive decline.
- Challenge your mind with puzzles, brain teasers, or strategic games.
- Read books, explore new subjects, or learn new skills to keep your mind sharp and engaged.[103]

Prioritizing self-care activities:

- Self-care is crucial for nurturing our overall well-being and maximizing our health span.

- Ensure you obtain adequate sleep to support proper rest and rejuvenation.[104]
- Practice stress management techniques like mindfulness, meditation, or engaging in hobbies you enjoy.[105]

WISDOM SPAN

While the uncertainty of our remaining Time weighs on us, this Time of our lives can be the most fun because if we have taken advantage of storing Time during the last twenty to thirty years, we are prepared for this next epoch. We are cruising into the future with a fair amount of accumulated wealth in all its forms and are ready to tackle this next phase.

As I explain this phase to my clients, I break it down into three overlapping stages: the Discovery Years, the Mastery Years, and the Legacy Years.

THE DISCOVERY YEARS (APPROXIMATELY AGES SIXTY-SIX–SEVENTY-SEVEN)

The Discovery Years represent the active retirement stage, typically lasting from the mid-sixties to the late seventies. Retirees pursuing new interests, traveling, and engaging in various activities characterize this stage. During the Discovery Years, active retirees often focus on:

- Travel and adventure
- Hobbies and creative pursuits
- Fitness and well-being
- Volunteering and giving back
- Social connections and support networks

The first year of retirement often feels like a vacation, in which the retiree has newfound freedom and Time to explore.[106]

As the vacation phase ends, retirees start to refocus on their ikigai. This reflection often leads to the pursuit of encore careers—second acts in retirement that combine passion, purpose, and income.[107] Examples of encore careers include:

- Teaching or mentoring
- Starting a small business or consultancy
- Nonprofit or community work
- Environmental or social activism
- Arts- and culture-related pursuits

"I love Sunday nights, knowing I have no travel, appointments, or deadlines facing me Monday morning is a great feeling."
—STEVE MCMANUS

THE MASTERY YEARS (APPROXIMATELY AGES SEVENTY-SEVEN–EIGHTY-EIGHT)

The Mastery Years span from the late seventies to the late eighties. During this time, retirees scale back their physical and travel activities, focusing more on family and close relationships. In this stage, priorities often shift to:

- Spending Time with family and friends
- Engaging in more leisurely hobbies
- Continuing personal development and lifelong learning
- Creating a lasting legacy

"It is at this point you realize how important those few people in your life are. Family and friends are dwindling, so enjoy them while you can. Also, remember to find doctors that are younger than you."

—TOM TONGUE

THE LEGACY YEARS (APPROXIMATELY AGES EIGHTY-EIGHT–NINETY-NINE)

The Legacy Years typically encompass the late eighties and beyond. This stage is often marked by increasing medical and emotional challenges, as well as a decline in mobility.[108] During the Legacy years, retirees and their families may need to:

- Adapt to changing health needs and mobility limitations
- Access appropriate medical care and support services
- Navigate the emotional challenges of aging, such as grief and loss
- Focus on maintaining quality of life and dignity

By understanding the Discovery, Mastery, and Legacy years, we can more effectively plan for and navigate this journey. Each stage presents unique opportunities and challenges, and by being prepared, we can maximize enjoyment and fulfillment during this stage of our lives.

HACK #12—BUILD A HEALTH SPAN TO MATCH YOUR LIFE SPAN

WEALTH SPAN

In the movie *The Martian*, Matt Damon's character, Mark Watney, finds himself stranded on Mars with limited food supplies after his crew leaves him behind during an emergency evacuation. To survive, he plans to stretch his rations until the next mission to Mars arrives in four years.

Watney understands his full-time job is to figure out how to make his resources last until he is rescued. His action plan includes:

- Staying active and mentally healthy—Watney exercises regularly to stay physically fit and maintains a positive attitude to stay mentally healthy. He keeps himself entertained by listening to music and watching old TV shows.
- Growing his food—Watney plans to use Martian soil, water, and waste as fertilizer. He creates a greenhouse where he grows potatoes, providing him with enough calories to survive.
- Conserving water—Watney realizes water is a precious resource on Mars and he needs to conserve it. He uses a system to extract water from the Martian atmosphere and recycles his urine to produce clean drinking water.
- Calculating the remaining food supply—Watney starts by calculating how much food he has left and how many calories he must consume daily to stay alive.

Fortunately, we are not being asked to recycle our urine to survive in retirement.

However, like Watney, we need to think of this stage of life as a business. This business has limited resources and income, and the goal is making these resources last for our remaining lifetime.

I hope you do not mind if I stretch this movie metaphor

a bit: staying active and healthy is the health span discussion, growing food is equivalent to a second career, and conserving water is maintaining important relationships.

The last item is to calculate the remaining food supply or, in our context, did we bank enough Time to get us through. Or, asked another way, how long will the money last?

This calculation can be daunting with an unknown end date. Most folks I talk to want to be sure they have enough but are not interested in leaving significant assets to the next generation.

Most understand they need a cushion in their later years, and most want to leave a little something to the next generation if there is any left. Most importantly, it is vital to many of my clients that they are not a burden on their children.

What are the steps to figure this out?

HOW MUCH IN INCOME

If the business you worked for came to you and said you no longer needed to come in to work but they would continue sending your paycheck for the rest of your life, you would likely take that deal without a lot of thought.

The reason is the amount deposited in the bank is what we rely on for our living expenses. This amount is our gross income minus several deductions, such as:

- Federal tax
- State and local tax
- Social Security and Medicare
- Retirement savings plan (like a 401(k) or 403(b))
- Other miscellaneous deductions

What I've found is over the years of going through this

exercise, most of us live on approximately 55–60 percent of our gross income. However, once you retire, taxes decrease (since you no longer contribute to Social Security), retirement plan contributions cease, and other deductions disappear.

Here's a hack to estimate how much you might need if you stopped working:

- Identify the net amount deposited into your checking account. For our example, let's say it's $2,000 per paycheck.
- Multiply this amount by the number of paychecks you receive annually. For instance, $2,000 × 24 = $48,000. This figure represents your annual living expenses.
- We divide this amount by 70 percent to account for taxes to calculate a pre-tax figure. Using our example, $48,000 divided by 70 percent equals $68,571.42.

Thus, someone with an annual gross income of about $80,000 needs approximately $69,000 to maintain their life-style without employment calculated as follows:

- (80,000 × 60 percent) = $48,000,
- $48,000 divided by 70 percent = $68,571.43 or rounded up $69,000.

It's important to remember that taxes are still applicable on earnings from investments or withdrawals from retirement plans.

This hack provides a ballpark figure for the income level someone may need. While this is a quick way to check if you're on track, it's essential to remember, you must consider numerous other variables. Generally, if your income remains consistent before and after retirement, you should be in good shape.

HOW MUCH IN ASSETS

Once we establish the necessary income level, we can calculate the requisite assets based on age. For the example given, asset requirements for individuals in their:

- Sixties equals $1.7 million (calculated by dividing $69,000 by 4 percent)
- Seventies equals $1.3 million (calculated by dividing $69,000 by 5 percent)
- Eighties equals $1.1 million (calculated by dividing $69,000 by 6 percent)

By having this amount in investments and taking a percentage of the account each year, the portfolio of assets will last for a lifetime.

However, the income will fluctuate. If the portfolio performs well, it will provide the required income. If the portfolio underperforms, the income may go down. How do you handle this?

HOW MUCH IS DISCRETIONARY?

Returning to the movie analogy of *The Martian*, there is a scene where the hatch blows off Watney's greenhouse, which ruins his crop.

An underperforming portfolio is like that, and we are going to have to finance the **** out of this to survive! (You'll get this reference if you saw the movie. If not, watch it!)

In finance, this is called a tail risk. Tail risk is an uncommon but potentially significant event in a statistical distribution's extreme ends, or "tails," usually beyond the normal range of outcomes. In finance and investing, tail risk refers to the probability of an investment portfolio experiencing extreme losses, often due to unpredictable and rare market events. To put it more simply, something really bad just happened!

As we operate this new environment of generating income from a portfolio, we must build fire breaks into our plan to manage adverse tail risks.

A fire break is a carefully created gap designed to slow down or halt the spread of destruction caused by a wildfire. Here, a bear market causes the wildfire of destruction in stocks. These fire breaks are:

Fire Break 1—Cash reserves = six months of required expenses, which are mortgage, utilities, food, and required debt services, such as car loans and minimum credit card payments.

Fire Break 2—Required expenses cannot exceed 75 percent of after-tax income.

By incorporating these two fire breaks into our strategy, most portfolios will survive "Black Swan" events. The portfolio survives because the required income can be reduced to essential expenses, and the cash reserves can carry the needed income when combined with a significantly reduced payment from the portfolio for quite some time.

ROCK'S MUSINGS

Nassim Taleb coined the term Black Swan event to describe an extremely rare and unpredictable event in the world of finance. Picture a serene pond where for the past fifty years, all you've ever seen are white swans. As an observer, you would think assuming that all swans are white would be safe. Then one day, a black swan appears. You could never have predicted it based on your experience, and its appearance dramatically changes your understanding of the world. A Black Swan event in the financial world is just as surprising and impactful. For instance, the global financial crisis of 2008 is considered a Black Swan event. Few predicted the collapse of major financial institutions and the subsequent economic downturn, making it an unexpected event with severe repercussions.

HOW MUCH IN OTHER INCOME?

Most have some other sources of guaranteed income. Social Security covers most Americans, and its benefit calculation is designed to be progressive, meaning it replaces a higher percentage of pre-retirement income for lower-income earners than for higher-income earners. This progressive structure aims to provide a more substantial safety net for those who have earned less over their working lives. It provides:

- Guaranteed benefits—Social Security provides guaranteed monthly benefits that adjust for inflation, ensuring beneficiaries maintain their purchasing power over time. This adjustment is crucial for lower-income earners with limited savings and investments to rely on during retirement or disability.
- Survivor and disability benefits—Lower-income earners and their families can also benefit from Social Security's provisions for survivors and disability benefits. These benefits provide financial support to surviving spouses, children, or disabled workers, helping to alleviate financial strain in times of need.
- Longevity protection—Since Social Security benefits are paid for a beneficiary's life, they offer protection against the risk of outliving one's savings. This benefit is especially important for lower-income earners who may have more limited financial resources to draw upon in retirement.

According to the Social Security Administration, for folks collecting this benefit, it represents about 30 percent of their total income.[109]

Using our example of a person who needs $69,000 per year of taxable income, the following is what is needed:

- ($69,000 Gross Income) − ($20,700 Social Security) = $48,300 Income from Investments
- Dividing $48,300 by 4 percent = $1.2 Million

Given this, the amount needed for someone in their sixties drops from about $1.7 million to about $1.2 million of accumulated assets to be comfortable into the future.

The same calculation can be made for other pensions from state governments, unions, lottery payouts, etc.

HACK #13—CALCULATE NEEDED INCOME AND ASSETS WITH YOUR PAYCHECK

TAKEAWAYS

While moving into this last epoch of life can be daunting, knowing and anticipating what lies ahead makes the journey more manageable and enjoyable.

The things to do during this stage are a continuation of the things that got us here. Maintain strong relationships, engage in physical activity, make managing the three phases of Discovery, Mastery, and Legacy a full-time job, and, finally, continue to search for or live your ikigai!

Again, it sounds easy, but moving through all these phases

of life and how you think about the future will impact your success in the future.

Having good mental models that help frame this future you imagine is critical.

"100 years old isn't just a number. It's a story of a journey, a saga of survival, and a testament to resilience."

—Unknown

CHAPTER 10

MENTAL MODELS, OR HOW TO THINK ABOUT TIME

Mental models serve as a framework that enables us to navigate complex situations, make informed decisions, and better understand the world. By providing a structured thinking approach, mental models empower individuals to process information efficiently, identify connections between seemingly unrelated concepts, and adapt to novel circumstances.

Warren Buffett uses a circle of competence mental model when choosing investments,[110] Elon Musk relies on a physics-first principals' mental model to make his discoveries,[111] and Steve Jobs was able to convince people of his way of thinking by using the reframing mental model.[112]

Understanding how to use Time effectively is critical to hacking the Time-Wealth Matrix. Mental models can be a guide for addressing the life-defining questions in each epoch by establishing a structure for introspection, prioritization, and setting objectives. Effectively using mental models involves:

- Identifying the suitable model for a given situation.
- Applying the model to scrutinize the problem.
- Adjusting one's perspective based on insights derived from the model.

Models that work well for hacking the uncertain future include:

- Hierarchy of needs—Abraham Maslow's hierarchy of needs is a motivational theory that organizes human needs into five tiers, in which lower-level needs must be satisfied before higher-level needs can be addressed. These tiers are physiological, safety, love, belonging, esteem, and self-actualization. This model can prioritize human needs and motivations in various contexts, from personal growth to organizational development.
- Working backward—This mental model entails starting with the end goal and working in reverse to pinpoint the necessary steps to achieve it. Working backward helps break down complex tasks into manageable components, leading to more effective planning and execution.
- Inversion—This is a premortem thinking by envisioning how this course of action goes wrong. It is identifying obstacles and potential solutions before they are needed. By considering what could go wrong or what should be avoided, inversion allows individuals to recognize potential pitfalls and develop strategies to overcome them.
- Margin of safety—Commonly employed in finance and engineering, the margin of safety concept requires incorpo-

rating a buffer into a decision to account for uncertainties and risks. By acknowledging the possibility of errors or unforeseen circumstances, this model encourages prudent decision-making that minimizes potential negative consequences.

- Diversification—Diversification involves spreading resources across multiple areas to manage risk and uncertainty. This mental model can be applied to various aspects of life, including investments, career choices, and personal relationships. Diversification reduces dependency on a single area and helps mitigate the impact of unexpected setbacks.

The following are examples for each model.

HIERARCHY OF NEEDS

- The hierarchy of needs, based on Maslow's model, is a powerful tool that individuals can use to prioritize their needs and goals in various aspects of life. Here are a few real-world examples of people implementing this model:
    - A college graduate starting their career may initially prioritize finding a stable job to fulfill their essential needs like food, shelter, and healthcare. Once these needs are met, they can then concentrate on establishing meaningful relationships with colleagues and friends. As they become more comfortable in their social and work environments, they can direct their efforts toward personal growth, such as pursuing further education or seeking professional development opportunities.
    - A single parent might prioritize providing for their children's basic needs like food, clothing, and a safe living

environment. As these necessities are addressed, the parent can work on fostering a loving and supportive family atmosphere and nurturing emotional connections with their children. Once these relational needs are met, the parent may pursue self-fulfillment goals, such as joining a community group or exploring personal interests.

We often overlook the basics in life. Have you ever stopped to think about what your most essential needs are? We all know we need food and shelter, but which comes first? And does it depend on what's more readily available?

Here's an exercise some might find helpful. Jot down the basic needs for a comfortable life. Then, write down the next level up for each item. It's an interesting exercise that can help define the progression of needs and wants. Here is an example for shelter:

- Level 0—Physiological: Living in a shared apartment in New York City with a bunch of roommates.
- Level 1—Esteem: Having your own apartment without any roommates.
- Level 2—Self-actualization: Owning a condo with a fantastic view and, of course, no roommates.

It's a simple way to break down needs and desires into manageable levels. Give it a try, and you might discover surprising things about your priorities and aspirations.

Here are some topics to think through:

- Physiological
  - Food
  - Water

- ◦ Shelter
- ◦ Sleep
- Safety
  - ◦ Security
  - ◦ Stability
  - ◦ Health
- Love/Belonging
  - ◦ Friendship
  - ◦ Family
  - ◦ Intimacy
- Esteem
  - ◦ Confidence
  - ◦ Achievement
  - ◦ Respect
- Self-Actualization
  - ◦ Creativity
  - ◦ Growth
  - ◦ Fulfillment

Using mental models, you can figure out what matters most at each stage of life and decide how to best allocate precious resources like Time and money. Sorting out the hierarchy of needs allows a person to layer on other mental models and craft a life that, when looked back on, genuinely makes them happy to have lived it.

WORKING BACKWARD

The next mental model to add to your toolkit is working backward.

A good example might be buying a new home. Before you sign the contract, imagine it's fifteen years from today, and you've just sold your home. Now, let's work backward to see what steps you took to make that happen. First, you'd have to have spent years maintaining and possibly even improving the property to make sure it retains its value or, better yet, increases in value. Improvements might have involved regular upkeep, renovations, or upgrades.

Next, you'd have to have thought about the financial aspects. You made sure to budget and plan for mortgage payments, property taxes, insurance, and maintenance costs. You might have refinanced your mortgage at some point to take advantage of better interest rates.

Going back further, when you first bought the home, you thoroughly researched the location, local amenities, and potential for future growth in the area. You took your time and negotiated a fair price that you felt confident would serve as a solid, long-term investment.

Before starting your home search, you took the crucial step of assessing your financial situation. You figured out how much you could afford, got pre-approved for a mortgage, and saved up for a down payment and closing costs.

By working backward from the end goal of selling your home in fifteen years, you can see the steps you need to take today and throughout the entire process. This mental model helps you stay focused on the big picture while ensuring you've prepared for the journey ahead.

INVERSION

While working backward is a best-case model, inversion can be considered a worst-case scenario approach. It's all about dodging problems by actively spotting them beforehand. Let's say you're considering making a significant life change, like moving for a new job. You could consider potential reasons you might be unhappy in the new situation—maybe a lack of friends or struggling to adjust to your new surroundings—and then devise a plan to tackle these challenges ahead of time.

Here's an example: What are the downsides of not having an emergency fund?

1. If I lose my job, how will I cover my rent?
2. What if my car breaks down, and I can't afford the repairs needed to drive to work?

Inversion is all about considering the worst-case scenario so you can plan for it over time. It's also a way to prepare for a bad outcome that may or may not happen.

Using the home purchase example, we can invert the process and think through what might create undue hardships for home ownership. These challenges may include zoning changes, redistricting of local schools, increased taxes, job changes that require a move, the loss of income, the size of the home for a growing family, and downsides to retiring in this location.

None of these things alone should stop the purchase, but as the saying goes, forewarned is forearmed.

The following list should help this brainstorming.

Time Frame: Age eighteen to thirty-three

- Potential Problems
  - Lack of professional direction—Many young adults face uncertainty about their career paths and the potential for unemployment.
  - Debt accumulation—Student loans, credit card debt, and other liabilities can become overwhelming.
  - Unanticipated health issues—One can still face serious health problems despite youth.

- Broken relationships—Breakups, divorce, or losing friendships can be devastating.
- Lack of self-identity—Struggling to understand oneself can lead to mental health issues, including anxiety and depression.
- Preparations
  - Look for internships, mentors, and career guidance.
  - Learn financial literacy, budgeting, and debt management.
  - Prioritize health with regular checkups, a balanced diet, and exercise; have health insurance.
  - Nurture relationships, but also develop personal resilience and coping mechanisms.
  - Seek self-understanding through reading, travel, hobbies, and therapy if needed.

Time Frame: Age thirty-four to sixty-six

- Potential Problems
  - Career stagnation—Not progressing professionally can lead to dissatisfaction and financial challenges.
  - Financial instability—Lack of savings or investment can lead to an uncertain future.
  - Health decline—Chronic diseases can become more prevalent.
  - Strained relationships—With children, spouses, or aging parents.
  - Lack of purpose—This can lead to a midlife crisis.
- Preparations
  - Seek continuous learning and professional development; be open to career transitions.

- Regularly save and invest for retirement; seek financial advice.
- Prioritize preventative healthcare and regular checkups; maintain a healthy lifestyle.
- Work on communication and compromise; seek professional help if needed.
- Engage in introspection and seek activities that provide satisfaction and meaning.

Time Frame: Age sixty-seven to ninety-nine

- Potential Problems
  - Insufficient retirement funds—This can lead to financial stress and reduced quality of life.
  - Health deterioration—Aging comes with increased health concerns and potential disability.
  - Loss of loved ones—This can lead to grief and loneliness.
  - Feeling of irrelevance—Difficulty in finding purpose post-retirement.
  - End-of-life anxieties—Fear and stress regarding mortality and legacy.
- Preparations
  - Plan for retirement early; consider diverse income sources.
  - Maintain regular health checkups; have a strong healthcare plan.
  - Develop a strong social network; engage in community activities.
  - Find purpose in mentoring, volunteering, or hobbies.
  - Discuss end-of-life decisions and legacy with family; consider psychological support if needed.

MARGIN OF SAFETY

Building a margin of safety into a plan allows bad things to happen without upsetting the apple cart. It is a prudent way of building plans.

Using our home purchase example, when you're searching for that perfect home, you'll want to consider the needs of a growing family. Having a margin of safety means not stretching your finances too thin.

Opt for a home well within your budget rather than pushing the limits of your mortgage pre-approval. Think about the location and future growth of the area. Be conservative in your appreciation estimates.

If there are two incomes with plans for kids, account for possible changes in your financial situation, like one parent taking time off work for parental leave or unforeseen childcare costs. Building a buffer in your budget will prepare you for unexpected expenses and life changes.

Fast forward to the fifteen-year mark when you're getting ready to sell your home; be mindful of market conditions. If the market isn't favorable for sellers, having a margin of safety built into your financial plan can provide the flexibility to wait for a better opportunity to sell compared to feeling pressured to sell at a less-than-ideal time.

The two fire breaks we established earlier also provide a safety cushion in case of a stock market downturn.

DIVERSIFICATION

Diversifying across all areas of your life when possible reduces the impact of the unexpected. A person can diversify through life in:

- Raising kids—For your children's education and extracurricular activities, diversify their experiences by encouraging them to take part in various sports, arts, and clubs. Diversifying will expose them to different interests and skills and help them become well-rounded individuals ready to adapt to different situations in life.

- Financial planning—Diversification is crucial when investing for your family's future and planning for retirement. Spread your investments across various asset classes, such as stocks, bonds, real estate, and cash, to minimize the risk of losses from any one area. One way to do this is by having a side hustle or even owning a rental property. Multiple streams of income can reduce your dependence on just one source and provide some financial security. Plus, having a little extra money coming in is always nice!
- Career planning—As a family, aim for diverse skillsets and job opportunities. Encourage continuous learning and skill development, which can help each family member adapt to changing job markets and protect against potential job losses. Diversified skills can also open doors to new opportunities and career paths.
- Insurance and emergency funds—Ensure you have a diversified approach to protecting your family against unexpected events. This includes having an emergency fund to cover at least three to six months of living expenses and various types of insurance, such as life, health, and property insurance, to safeguard your family's well-being and financial stability.

An individual can apply the concept of diversification to various aspects of their life, such as acquiring skills in different fields to enhance career prospects, nurturing a variety of social connections to build a robust support network, and pursuing multiple hobbies to cultivate a well-rounded and fulfilling life.

One of the most valuable pieces of advice I didn't follow came from my colleague Andrew when I shared I was considering pursuing an advanced degree in finance. With a chuckle, he suggested I might be better off learning to operate a backhoe just in case this finance path didn't pan out.

His point was that when you're wholly invested in a single field (or investment, location, or activity), you become vulnerable to its risks and uncertainties.

There are various examples of this:

- In business, Kodak was once a leading company in the photography industry, but its inability to adapt to the digital revolution led to its eventual downfall.
- What will professional athletes do once their careers end?
- I've had clients who were over-invested in individual stocks in companies that went bankrupt; those who followed my advice to diversify are still financially well off. Others who did not diversify have not been so lucky.
- Focusing exclusively on one aspect of health, such as diet or exercise, while neglecting mental well-being, sleep, and stress management, can lead to an imbalanced and unhealthy lifestyle.

MENTAL MODELS—BENEFITS AND LIMITATIONS

The benefits and limitations of using mental models for decision-making and problem-solving on a personal level include:

BENEFITS

- Improved self-awareness—Mental models can help individuals understand their values, motivations, and priorities.

- Enhanced decision-making—By providing a structured-thinking approach, mental models can lead to better personal decisions.
- Adaptability—Mental models can help individuals identify patterns and adapt to new situations or challenges.
- Reduced stress—Using mental models can make complex decisions more manageable, leading to reduced stress and anxiety.

LIMITATIONS

- Over-reliance—Depending too much on mental models may prevent individuals from considering alternative perspectives or exploring new ideas.
- Misapplication—Using an inappropriate mental model for a particular situation can lead to poor decisions or unintended consequences.
- Confirmation bias—Mental models may unknowingly reinforce preexisting beliefs or preferences, hindering objective decision-making.
- Incomplete information—The effectiveness of mental models relies on the accuracy and completeness of the data used to inform decisions.

OTHER MENTAL MODELS

Other mental models that individuals can use to improve their understanding and decision-making skills include:

- The Pareto principle (80/20 Rule)—Focus on the most impactful 20 percent of tasks that yield 80 percent of the results.

- Occam's razor—Choose the simplest explanation for the evidence.
- Confirmation bias—Be aware of the tendency to seek information that confirms preexisting beliefs.

Sure, mental models aren't flawless, but they're good enough to give life a clear roadmap. By applying these models, you can do your best to foresee potential outcomes and likely landmines to avoid and make choices based on the information you've got.

HACK #14—USE MENTAL MODELS TO PROJECT THE FUTURE.

TAKEAWAYS

The world comes at us fast, and information in context is an asset. Putting that information in a form relevant to our situation helps us make good decisions. Knowing we have a margin of safety prevents cognitive fear of loss from taking over. Outlining worst-case scenarios with the inversion mental model puts today's news into context.

Using the proper tools to hack the Matrix is vital.

The proper tool that will help us is crafting a mental map that gets us from here to there.

"Modeling is a tool; it's not a representation of the world, it's a representation of your understanding."

—UNKNOWN

CHAPTER 11

BUILDING LINES TO CONQUER TIME

The future is both exciting and overwhelming. Sit for a moment and think about how your life story will be written over the next ten, twenty, and thirty years.

No, really, stop reading, and take a moment to think about your life.

No, really!

Okay, welcome back.

Now let me ask you some questions.

- How much time did you spend on this exercise?
- Where did you start?
    - Job?
    - Kids?
    - Money?
    - Vacations?
    - Somewhere else entirely?

Is it a jumbled mess in your mind, or was there an organized underlying theme?

In our postindustrial world ruled by the clock, our lives are complicated with choices.

Not that our ancestors had it easy, but some things were a given, for instance, the decision of whom to marry. Many societies practiced arranged marriages, for which parents, not the betrothed, were the decisive voices. Love often took a back seat to social standing, financial stability, or family alliances. Similarly, the choice of career wasn't a choice. Occupations were usually inherited—if your father was a blacksmith, you would likely become a blacksmith. As for religion, most societies held mono-religious belief systems, so the religion you were born into was the religion you followed. Finally, consider residence. Many lived their entire lives within a few miles of their birthplaces: resources, and the sheer difficulty of long-distance travel, limited mobility.

So, having many choices is a good thing, but how do we choose from all the available options and then prioritize them?

Well, looking at Leonardo da Vinci's inventions or J. K. Rowling's complex world of *Harry Potter* as examples, the question arises: how did they keep track of all their ideas?

Well, they wrote down their ideas. Rowling is known for keeping complex charts of her ideas with storylines mapped out. Da Vinci had his notebooks that he scribbled in (if only I could scribble like da Vinci!) to keep the ideas flowing.

Many successful people use a technique known as mind mapping to think through their complex plans. A mind map visualizes ideas, concepts, or information organized around a central topic or theme. It is a powerful tool for brainstorming, planning, organizing, and problem-solving as it helps individuals to think creatively and explore connections between seemingly unrelated ideas.

To create a mind map, you start by placing the main topic or central idea in the center of a blank page. You draw branches that radiate outward from there, connecting to subtopics or related concepts. These subtopics can further branch into smaller, more specific ideas or details. The branches often represent categories or relationships, and they can be color-coded, labeled, or adorned with images to enhance visual appeal and facilitate understanding.

The benefits of using a mind map include:

- Enhanced creativity—Mind mapping encourages the free flow of ideas and stimulates creative thinking by allowing you to explore multiple possibilities and connections.
- Improved memory and retention—The visual nature of mind maps aids in memory retention as it helps you create mental associations between ideas, making it easier to recall information later.
- Better organization and understanding—By visually organizing information in a hierarchical and interconnected manner, mind maps help you identify patterns, relationships, and priorities more easily.
- Effective problem-solving—Mind maps can break down complex problems into smaller, more manageable components, allowing for a better understanding of the issue and the development of more effective solutions.
- Increased productivity—Mind maps can streamline planning and decision-making processes, leading to more efficient use of Time and resources.

A mind map is a visual tool that helps individuals explore, organize, and understand complex ideas and information by representing them in a structured, interconnected format. Using mind maps to bring all the topics of wealth together will provide the tools needed to organize all the many decisions made over a lifetime.

In our context of wealth, let's mind map the Wealth Equation.

WEALTH EQUATION MIND MAP

Here is a visualization starting with the five major topics.

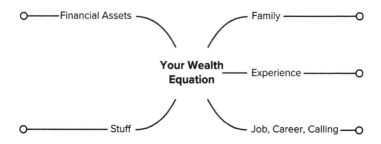

Family

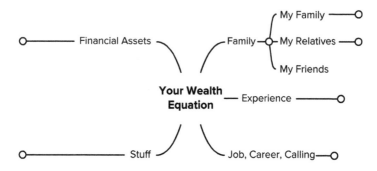

We can then think about how the future might unfold. Let's focus on My Family and pick Ryan.

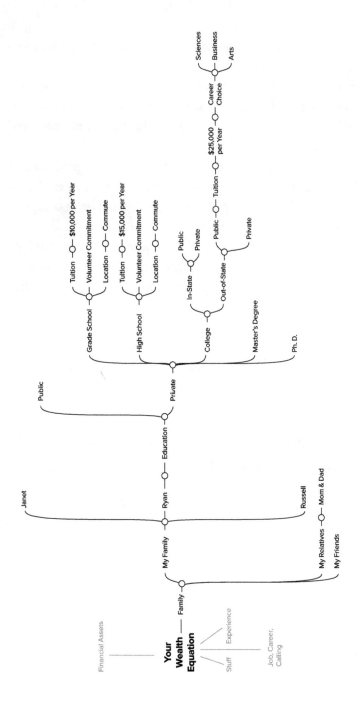

Using mind mapping, we have organized future decisions more consciously.

This map assumes Ryan has yet to start grade school, and the decision facing us is sending him to public or private school. If we go private, what are the various financial and time commitments?

Continuing, we can compare choices about high school, college, and post-graduate degrees. Depending on where Ryan's talents lie, it might impact what he will focus on in college.

Are we sure of these answers? No, probably not.

However, some things will become obvious as we build out the future. For example, Ryan and Russell are two years apart in age. Where will the funding come from for the years they overlap in college?

We see this as a pinch point in the future and determine ways to address it decades ahead of needing the funds.

We continue to work through the Wealth Equation based on what we know today.

EXPERIENCES, KNOWLEDGE, WISDOM

What does our future look like as we build out experience and education?

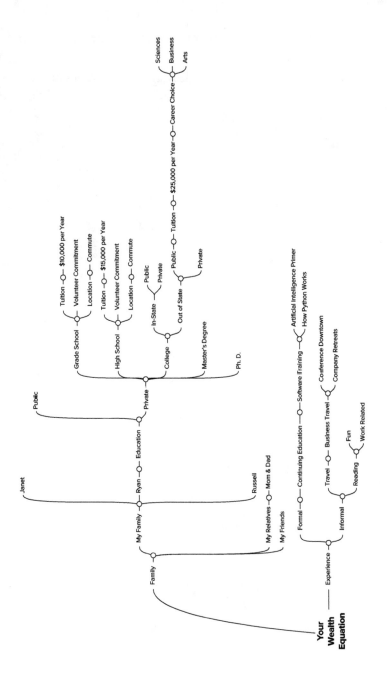

Just like a roadmap, it becomes more cluttered as it covers more ground.

Fortunately, like with Google Maps, we can zoom in when needed:

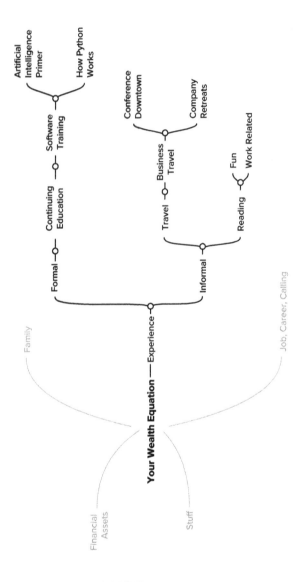

Here we can think through the short-term and long-term future regarding education, company retreats for networking, reading, and continuing education.

This empowers us to be strategic in deciphering what might be valuable personally and professionally as we move through the various epochs of our lives.

JOB, CAREER, CALLING

As we continue to solve for the answer to the Wealth Equation, future Time takes shape. Mapping is a powerful tool that allows us to see a bigger picture.

Now we can think more holistically about what important future decisions we will need to make and when. Scouting out the path allows us to prepare better.

Equally important, as we look out over the next five to ten years, our priorities begin to bubble to the surface. If we had unlimited Time and money, we would do it all, but this exercise will help us visualize and rank our priorities and use of these limited resources.

And since most decisions have opportunity costs, we can weigh these costs relative to our priorities.

For example, our ideal position is Sr. Vice President in North America. What does the path to this role look like, and what other priorities might suffer? What additional education is involved? What are the steps between our current position and this role? Will there be Time away from family, and will relocation be required?

Again, zoom in:

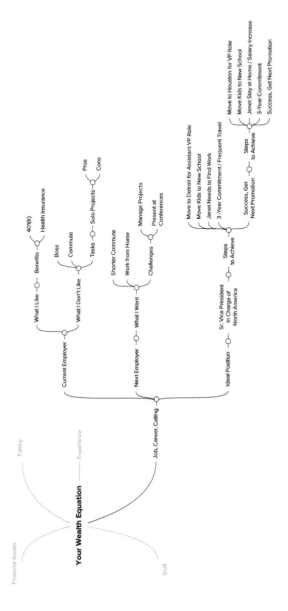

Seeing the bigger picture allows us to effectively manage the many parts of our lives and make better jump/no-jump decisions based on using the previously discussed mental models.

FINANCIAL ASSETS

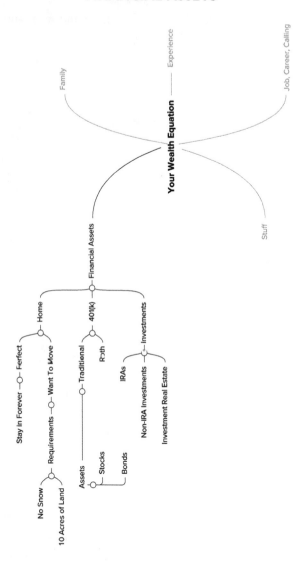

With this information, we can build out an investment pro-file looking at both the location of assets and the risk/return profile to more closely match our priorities over time.

STUFF

We can also integrate all the stuff we need and want and add it to the list in a more holistic way.

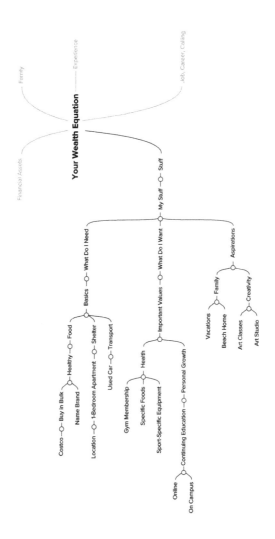

Putting all the individual pieces together, the Wealth Equation falls into place.

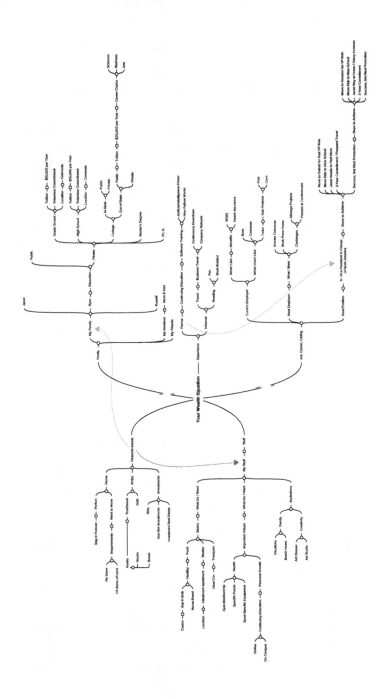

$$\text{Wealth} = FF + EKW + J + S + FA + T$$

(Family, Friends, Experience, Knowledge, Wisdom, Job, Stuff, Financial Assets, Time)

Since our lives are complicated, and all the parts impact all the other parts, we can use a mind map to connect these different areas of our lives.

Paying for a kid's education and getting the stuff we want will require money. How do we balance this? Our ideal job might require additional education. Is this formal or informal? When do we accomplish this training?

Which one takes precedence? Another way of looking at it is like this: one person's Maserati is another person's college education.

Like the Wealth Equation and the Matrix, priorities are personalized.

We need to structure the future to achieve our wealth priorities.

PRIORITIES, MILESTONES, SYSTEMS

Navigating the future is akin to plotting a great ocean adventure. There will be a plethora of experiences to embrace but a finite period in which to engage with them. So, how do we schedule the future?

The key lies in understanding priorities, setting milestones, and establishing systems that guide the journey.

Picture priorities as a compass—they give you direction. Are you aiming for financial stability? Are you considering a comprehensive education for your kids? Or possibly nurturing closer relationships within the family?

Once you've established your compass points, we turn

to milestones—these are your waypoints, tangible markers showing your progress. A new house, your child's high school graduation, or a family trip worldwide could be among them. But how do we navigate from one waypoint to another?

That's where your systems, or your "ship," come into play. A well-structured routine, balanced lifestyle, or effective financial plan—these transport you toward your milestones. Like any long voyage, some systems operate in the background to get us safely from here to there:

- Crew management—Maintaining and improving relationships with friends and family.
- Emergency protocols or lifeboats—Cash reserves; health, disability, and life insurance; liability insurance; risk minimization; and avoidance strategies.
- Weather monitoring—Being aware of slow-moving disasters and battening down the hatches or, better yet, steering to avoid them—possible layoffs, health problems, debt accumulation, and knowledge obsolescence.
- Power systems—Job, career, or calling, finding our ikigai— what we do for work that allows us to support ourselves and our families and move our lives forward.
- Life support systems—Savings and investments to build up a bank of Time that allows us to focus on things that are truly important to us and to pass on Time to the people we love.
- Ballast systems—Understanding where stuff fits into our life. Being able to add things that smooth the journey but being able to throw things overboard when needed to protect the crew members.

Let's get to planning the voyage. (I think I've stretched this analogy far enough!)

This type of planning is very hierarchal. Let's figure out the most important things, put them in order, and allocate resources.

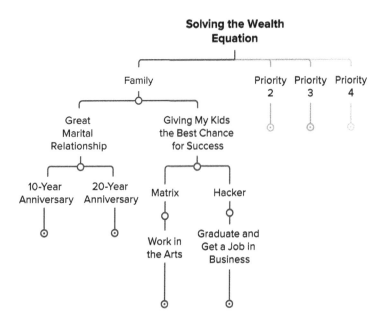

To build this out a bit, let's focus on family.

The number one priority is family, which is further broken down into the three family members of the spouse and two kids, Matrix and Hacker. We might define the milestones along the way as wedding anniversaries and a successful life launch for the two kids.

Once we've established priorities and milestones, we need to back into what we need to do to make them happen. Allocating funds allows us to hit the milestones that inform our priorities.

Solving the Wealth Equation

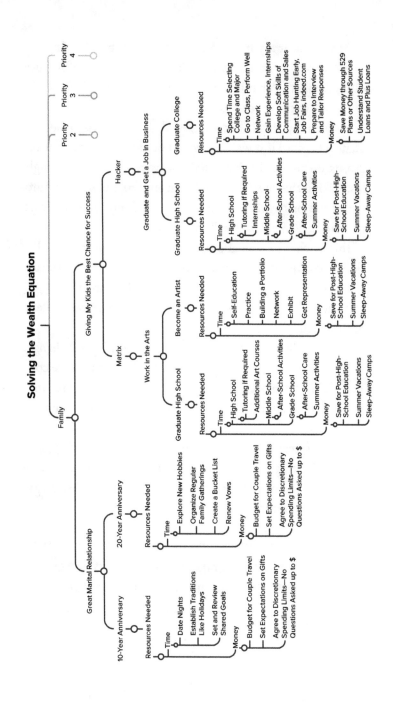

Again, I hear my friend Kevin, "Says easy, but does hard."

What is Priority 1, and how do I choose? What if my priorities conflict? What if priorities change? What if…?

The answers are yes, yes, and yes.

Fortunately, this is not a one-and-done exercise. I say fortunately because if it was, life would be extraordinarily boring. Also, we do not need to have all the answers as we work through this. Asking the questions will begin engaging with the future.

Let me bring back an earlier quote from Thomas Frey: *Thinking about the future will cause it to change.*

This is what I mean about not needing all the answers. By asking these questions, you alter the future to your will instead of leaving your future to chance, luck, fate, or kismet.

By actively engaging with the future, you will more likely encounter the future you want.

Over the three epochs of our lives, our priorities will change. We'll travel past waypoints and achieve milestones. As we continue along the chosen course, new challenges will arise, and we will have to alter the course to accommodate our changing futures.

By using readily available online tools for mind mapping and flowcharting, one can begin developing personal priorities, milestones, waypoints, and, finally, an informed strategy to manage the future.

HACK #15—USE MIND MAPPING TOOLS TO IMAGINE AND PRIORITIZE THE FUTURE

TAKEAWAYS

I stumbled upon this story and thought it might be appropriate here.[113]

A successful businessman was on vacation, walking along the beach in a small coastal village. He noticed a fisherman docked by the shore with a pile of fish. Intrigued, the businessman approached the fisherman and asked, "Why aren't you out there fishing more?"

The fisherman looked up and replied, "Because I've caught enough for today."

"Why don't you stay out longer and catch more?" the businessman inquired.

The fisherman responded, "What would I do with them?"

"You could sell them and make more money," the businessman suggested. "With that, you could fix up your boat, hire other fishermen, and expand your operations. Eventually, you could open your own processing plant, manage the product distribution, and build a brand."

"And then what?" asked the fisherman.

The businessman explained, "Then, you could move to a big city and manage your vast enterprise."

"And how long would all this take?" asked the fisherman.

"Perhaps 15 to 20 years," replied the businessman.

"And then what?" the fisherman asked again.

The businessman chuckled, "That's the best part. You could then sell your company stocks, become very rich, retire, and do whatever you want."

"And what would I want?" asked the fisherman.

The businessman smiled, "You could sleep late, fish a little, play with your kids, take a siesta with your wife, stroll into the village each evening, play the guitar with your amigos, and enjoy a carefree life."

The fisherman looked at the businessman, smiled, and said, "That's what I'm already doing."

In a fashion, both the fisherman and the businessman just performed a mind map by asking and answering a question: "And then what?"

My experience tells me the businessman and fisherman each found their ikigai at the end.

How is this?

It is unlikely that the businessman in this story will ever sleep late; he will always be trying to grow something bigger. He certainly would not try to convert someone to improve their business unless it was something he was anxious to share with others. His ikigai is seeing opportunity and then growing the opportunity into something bigger.

Alternatively, the fisherman has located his happy space and reason for being in a little village with his friends and family; he recognizes it, and he cannot be tempted by money.

Mind mapping and prioritization is not about trying to

micromanage your life, though it will help point out some things you should consider.

Instead, it is about creatively thinking about your future and visualizing the people, things, and life you want in a constantly changing world. With this information, current priorities can be formed, milestones mapped, and an engaged course of action can be taken, whether this is running an international business or operating a small fishing boat off the coast of somewhere hot.

Being actively engaged with our futures allows us to reach our final destination safely and in a manner we control.

"The future is not something we enter. The future is something we create."

—LEONARD I. SWEET

CHAPTER 12

CLOSING THE BOOKS

As we turn the final pages, let's reflect, aligning with Rovelli's insight: our lives are about evolving, not just existing. Our path has been marked by distinct phases—learning, accumulating, and ultimately, withdrawing and then passing—each year adding another chapter to our life's story.

Recall the essence of the Wealth Equation: Wealth is a composite of family, friends, experiences, knowledge, wisdom, jobs, possessions, financial assets, and the most important asset, Time. This equation isn't just a formula; it's a map to guide you through life's complexities, helping you balance and integrate these components into a harmonious whole.

While our actions may seem significant in life, afterward they eventually fade. It is time to "close the books" on our Personal Wealth Era.

Wealth Era — End of Epoch III

Account	Asset	Liability
Parents	0	0
Siblings	0	0
Friends	0	0
Children	33	0
Grandchildren	99	
Mentorships	10	0
Experiences	0	0
Knowledge	0	0
Wisdom	20	0
Things/Stuff	0	0
Financial Assets	33	0
Time	<u>0</u>	<u>0</u>
Total	**195**	0
Net Worth		**195**

While finite for each of us, Time leaves a lasting echo through the assets, relationships, and mentorships we leave behind.

If done well, our legacy is celebrated in heartfelt toasts and cherished memories.

Thankfully for us, this accounting remains in the future. As you move forward from here to that future, remember the true barrier to achieving wealth is often the reflection in the mirror. Embrace the journey with courage, cherishing time, valuing relationships, and seeking experiences that enrich your soul. Let your possessions be a means, not an end, and find joy in pursuing your calling.

Remember, wealth is personal; do not let others dictate what wealth is for you.

Learn how Time is the controlling variable in our lives. Manage Time.

Understand how your family and friends fit into your life and treasure important relationships. Small investments of time in friends and family reap huge rewards.

Experience life to the fullest. Say yes to adventure. Do not be afraid to say, "I do not know; can you help me?" Learn from books, but gain wisdom from being with and watching other people.

Get some stuff that makes you happy, but jettison stuff that does not. Own your stuff; do not let your stuff own you.

Find your ikigai.

Understand your value to the business world, get paid fairly with that value, and save Time so you can spend Time doing the other things you love to do with the people you love.

Financial assets are tools, not goals. They are important, but only to the extent they allow you to live the life you want.

Hack the Time-Wealth Matrix to discover the solution to your personal Wealth Equation:

$$\text{Wealth} = \text{Family} + \text{Friends} + \text{Experience} + \text{Knowledge} + \text{Wisdom} + \text{Job} + \text{Stuff} + \text{Financial Assets} + \text{Time}$$

The solution you find is personal, but the result is Real Wealth in a World of Fake Money.

APPENDIX

HACK THE TIME-WEALTH MATRIX

Hack #1—Teach kids about Time, money, currency, and family.

Helping children learn about value, currency, savings, and family will help them understand life's priorities. Do not outsource this to the internet and the advertisers.

Hack #2—Graduate in the top 50 percent, learn un-robotizable skills, save 10 percent of your income, get married, then have kids.

Take advantage of education and set yourself up for job success. Technology will replace skills, so learn ones that can't be replaced, and make life easier by following the success formula.

Hack #3—Protect 95 percent with 5 percent and ninety days of cash reserves.

Bad things happen to good people; protect yourself and your family with the right type of insurance: disability, life, car, renter, home, and liability.

Hack #4—Family close, good friends closer.

Throughout your life, your friends, and family will be your most important asset for health and companionship; treat them as such.

Hack #5—Have a plan to seek experience, knowledge, and wisdom.

Wisdom isn't just given to you. Get a plan together to get some on your own. Ask for mentorships and listen to podcasts. Keep learning.

Hack #6—Keep your agreements and discover your ikigai.

Be impeccable with your word, don't take anything personally, don't make assumptions, and always do your best. Keeping your agreements will lead you to the things you love.

Hack #7—Build a thing/stuff framework.

Understand what is valuable to you and surround yourself with these things.

Hack #8—Accumulate to be comfortable, and understand your comfortable.

It is our nature to want more, but more may not make you more comfortable. Know when you have enough.

Hack #9—Put your assets in the way of things that compound.

Be optimistic about the future; do not entertain the apocalypse. Invest your assets as an owner of the future.

Hack #10—Partner with Time to use the Rule of 72 to your advantage.

Money is math; saving is a choice. Take advantage of your doubling blocks.

Hack #11—Relationships compound. Invest in them regularly.

Identify the fifteen most important people in your life. Be there for them, and they will be there for you.

Hack #12—Build a health span to match your life span.

Get up, move, eat fresh food, and go to the doctor. You know what to do; do it.

Hack #13—Calculate needed income and assets with a paycheck.

You need your current after-tax income to be comfortable; use this amount to figure out your required assets.

Hack #14—Use mental models to project the future.

Use the hierarchy of needs, working backward, inversion, margin of safety, diversification.

Hack #15—Use mind mapping tools to imagine and prioritize the future.

Thinking about the future changes the future for the better. Mind map the possibilities.

SAVINGS APPENDIX

Earlier in the book, we discussed Matrix's saving strategy.

Matrix saves $1,750 per year (5 percent of his $35,000 income) plus 33 percent of any pay above the starting salary of $35,000. After thirty-three years, Matrix had accumulated more than a million dollars.

Strategies revolve around an amount saved that escalates with income over time.

Money Is Math/Savings Is a Choice

Save $41 per month starting at age 21. Increase the monthly amount by 10% every January. Earn 7% Annually/3% Annual Pay Increase. The December value shows the total of the account as the years go by. What starts as **$508** in the first year grows to over **$1,000,000 at age 66.**

Age	Salary	Saved Monthly	Saved Annually	% of Annual Income	J	F	M	A	M	J	J	A	S	O	N	D
21	35,000	41.00	492	1%	41	82	124	165	207	250	292	335	378	421	464	508
22	36,050	45.10	541	2%	556	605	653	702	751	801	850	901	951	1,002	1,052	1,104
23	37,132	49.61	595	2%	1,160	1,216	1,273	1,330	1,387	1,445	1,503	1,561	1,620	1,679	1,739	1,798
24	38,245	54.57	655	2%	1,863	1,929	1,995	2,061	2,127	2,194	2,262	2,330	2,398	2,466	2,535	2,605
25	39,393	60.03	720	2%	2,680	2,755	2,832	2,908	2,985	3,063	3,140	3,219	3,298	3,377	3,457	3,537
30	45,667	96.68	1,160	3%	9,019	9,168	9,318	9,469	9,621	9,774	9,928	10,082	10,238	10,394	10,552	10,710
35	52,941	155.70	1,868	4%	21,192	21,472	21,753	22,035	22,319	22,605	22,893	23,182	23,473	23,766	24,060	24,356
40	61,373	250.75	3,009	5%	43,582	44,087	44,595	45,106	45,620	46,137	46,657	47,179	47,705	48,234	48,767	49,302
45	71,148	403.84	4,846	7%	83,588	84,480	85,376	86,278	87,185	88,098	89,016	89,939	90,867	91,801	92,740	93,685
50	82,480	650.39	7,805	9%	153,614	155,161	156,716	158,281	159,855	161,437	163,030	164,631	166,242	167,862	169,491	171,130
55	95,617	1,047.45	12,569	13%	274,325	276,972	279,635	282,314	285,008	287,718	290,444	293,186	295,944	298,717	301,507	304,314
60	110,846	1,686.94	20,243	18%	479,975	484,462	488,975	493,514	498,080	502,672	507,292	511,938	516,611	521,311	526,039	530,795
65	128,501	2,716.83	32,602	25%	827,119	834,661	842,247	849,877	857,551	865,270	873,035	880,844	888,699	896,600	904,547	912,540
66	132,356	2,988.51	35,862	27%	920,852	929,212	937,621	946,079	954,586	963,143	971,750	980,407	989,115	997,873	1,006,683	1,015,543

Total Saved $389,563

Total Value $1,015,543

Money Is Math/Savings Is a Choice

Delay Savings until age 33/Save $154 per month. Increase the monthly amount by 10% every January.

Earn 7% Annually/3% Annual Pay Increase.

The December value shows the total of the account as the years go by. What starts as $1,908 in the first year grows to over $1,000,000 at age 66.

Age	Salary	Saved Monthly	Saved Annually	% of Annual Income	J	F	M	A	M	J	J	A	S	O	N	D
33	49,902	154.00	1,848	4%	154	309	465	621	779	938	1,097	1,257	1,419	1,581	1,744	1,908
34	51,399	169.40	2,033	4%	2,089	2,271	2,453	2,637	2,822	3,008	3,195	3,383	3,572	3,762	3,953	4,146
35	52,941	186.34	2,236	4%	4,356	4,568	4,781	4,995	5,211	5,427	5,645	5,865	6,085	6,307	6,530	6,755
40	61,373	300.10	3,601	6%	22,379	22,810	23,243	23,679	24,117	24,558	25,001	25,447	25,896	26,347	26,801	27,257
45	71,148	483.32	5,800	8%	57,822	58,643	59,468	60,299	61,134	61,974	62,818	63,668	64,523	65,383	66,247	67,117
50	82,480	778.39	9,341	11%	123,999	125,501	127,012	128,531	130,059	131,596	133,142	134,697	136,261	137,834	139,417	141,009
55	95,617	1,253.60	15,043	16%	243,472	246,146	248,836	251,541	254,262	256,999	259,751	262,520	265,305	268,106	270,924	273,758
60	110,846	2,018.94	24,227	22%	454,165	458,833	463,529	468,251	473,002	477,780	482,586	487,420	492,282	497,173	502,092	507,040
65	128,501	3,251.52	39,018	30%	819,401	827,432	835,510	843,636	851,808	860,029	868,297	876,614	884,979	893,393	901,856	910,368
66	132,356	3,576.67	42,920	32%	919,255	928,194	937,185	946,229	955,325	964,475	973,677	982,934	992,244	1,001,609	1,011,028	1,020,503

Total Saved $453,641

Total Value $1,020,503

Money Is Math/Savings Is a Choice

Save 6% per month starting at age 21/amount increases with 3% pay raise each year. Earn 7% Annually.

The December value shows the total of the account as the years go by. What starts as $2,048 in the first year grows to over $1,000,000 at age 66.

Age	Salary	Saved Monthly	Saved Annually	% of Annual Income	J	F	M	A	M	J	J	A	S	O	N	D
21	35,000	165.28	1,983	6%	165	332	499	667	836	1,006	1,177	1,350	1,523	1,697	1,872	2,048
22	36,050	180.25	2,163	6%	2,240	2,434	2,628	2,824	3,020	3,218	3,417	3,618	3,819	4,021	4,225	4,430
23	37,132	185.66	2,228	6%	4,642	4,854	5,068	5,283	5,500	5,718	5,937	6,157	6,379	6,601	6,826	7,051
24	38,245	191.23	2,295	6%	7,283	7,517	7,752	7,989	8,226	8,466	8,706	8,948	9,192	9,437	9,683	9,931
25	39,393	196.96	2,364	6%	10,185	10,442	10,700	10,959	11,220	11,482	11,746	12,012	12,279	12,547	12,818	13,089
30	45,667	228.34	2,740	6%	29,387	29,787	30,189	30,593	31,000	31,409	31,821	32,235	32,651	33,070	33,491	33,915
35	52,941	264.70	3,176	6%	58,988	59,597	60,209	60,825	61,444	62,067	62,694	63,325	63,959	64,597	65,238	65,883
40	61,373	306.86	3,682	6%	103,711	104,623	105,540	106,462	107,390	108,324	109,262	110,207	111,156	112,112	113,072	114,039
45	71,148	355.74	4,269	6%	170,311	171,660	173,017	174,382	175,755	177,136	178,525	179,922	181,328	182,741	184,163	185,593
50	82,480	412.40	4,949	6%	268,434	270,412	272,402	274,404	276,417	278,441	280,478	282,527	284,587	286,660	288,744	290,841
55	95,617	478.08	5,737	6%	411,836	414,716	417,614	420,528	423,459	426,407	429,373	432,355	435,356	438,373	441,408	444,461
60	110,846	554.23	6,651	6%	620,111	624,282	628,478	632,698	636,943	641,213	645,508	649,827	654,172	658,543	662,938	667,360
65	128,501	642.50	7,710	6%	921,145	927,161	933,212	939,298	945,420	951,577	957,770	964,000	970,266	976,568	982,907	989,283
66	132,356	661.78	7,941	6%	995,716	1,002,186	1,008,694	1,015,240	1,021,824	1,028,446	1,035,107	1,041,807	1,048,546	1,055,325	1,062,142	1,069,000

Total Saved $202,536

Total Value $1,069,000

Money Is Math/Savings Is a Choice

Delay until Age 33, Save 11% per month/amount increases with 3% pay raise each year. Earn 7% Annually.

The December value shows the total of the account as the years go by. What starts as $5,668 in the first year grows to over $1,000,000 at age 66.

Age	Salary	Saved Monthly	Saved Annually	% of Annual Income	J	F	M	A	M	J	J	A	S	O	N	D
33	49,902	457.36	5,488	11%	457	917	1,380	1,846	2,314	2,785	3,258	3,734	4,214	4,696	5,180	5,668
34	51,399	471.08	5,653	11%	6,172	6,679	7,189	7,702	8,218	8,737	9,259	9,784	10,313	10,844	11,378	11,916
35	52,941	485.22	5,823	11%	12,470	13,028	13,589	14,154	14,722	15,293	15,867	16,445	17,026	17,611	18,199	18,790
40	61,373	562.50	6,750	11%	54,501	55,382	56,267	57,158	58,054	58,955	59,861	60,773	61,690	62,612	63,540	64,473
45	71,148	652.09	7,825	11%	119,950	121,302	122,662	124,029	125,405	126,789	128,180	129,580	130,988	132,404	133,829	135,261
50	82,480	755.95	9,071	11%	219,531	221,568	223,616	225,677	227,749	229,834	231,930	234,039	236,160	238,294	240,440	242,598
55	95,617	876.35	10,516	11%	368,582	371,609	374,653	377,715	380,794	383,892	387,008	390,142	393,294	396,464	399,653	402,861
60	110,846	1,015.93	12,191	11%	589,018	593,470	597,948	602,452	606,982	611,539	616,122	620,732	625,369	630,033	634,724	639,442
65	128,501	1,177.75	14,133	11%	912,106	918,604	925,141	931,715	938,328	944,979	951,669	958,398	965,167	971,975	978,822	985,710
66	132,356	1,213.08	14,557	11%	992,673	999,677	1,006,721	1,013,807	1,020,934	1,028,102	1,035,312	1,042,565	1,049,860	1,057,197	1,064,577	1,072,000

Total Saved $316,843

Total Value $1,072,200

There are several ways to save for the future, but the longer you wait, the more you need to save annually to achieve the goal.

The secret to getting financial wealth is to be consistent, put funds in the way of higher-earning investments, and remember the Rule of 72 to take advantage of your remaining doubling zones.

ACKNOWLEDGMENTS

These people have made the book so much better by reading it and offering their thoughts, ideas, and criticisms. Thank you: Cathy Kalweit, Kevin Quinn, John Steinberg, Mike Warner, Andy Palmer, and Philip Costopoulos.

While I have written these ideas down, my colleagues have helped me shape them over the years. I value both their professionalism and their friendship through those years. They were always patient as I asked the hated question, "But why?" Thank you, Rey Roy, Jan Kowal, and Ed Moore.

To Ric and Jean Edelman, thank you for taking me in all those years ago and showing me what was possible when you put people first. Your impact on my family, millions of listeners, readers, and viewers is incalculable. The ripples in your pond continue to move outward. And that's the Truth About That!

Finally, to my clients, thank you for taking me into your life and trusting me with your future. It is an honor beyond words; know that none of this would be possible without you.

NOTES

1   Dictionary.com, s.v. "Wealth," accessed January 13, 2023, https://www.dictionary.com/browse/wealth.

2   Vicki A. Freedman and Brenda C. Spillman, "Disability and Care Needs among Older Americans," *Milbank Quarterly* 92, no. 3 (September 2014): 509–41, https://www.ncbi.nlm.nih.gov/pmc/articles/PMC4221755/.

3   Mayo Clinic Staff, "Friendships: Enrich Your Life and Improve Your Health," Mayo Clinic, January 12, 2022, https://www.mayoclinic.org/healthy-lifestyle/adult-health/in-depth/friendships/art-20044860.

4   University of Notre Dame, "Your Circle of Friends Is More Predictive of Your Health, Study Finds," ScienceDaily, June 17, 2019, https://www.sciencedaily.com/releases/2019/06/190617110533.htm.

5   Tamim Alnuweiri, "The Secret to Living Forever Just May Be the Quality of Your Friendships," Well+Good, July 3, 2017, https://www.wellandgood.com/friendship-key-to-living-longer/.

6   Catherine Clifford, "9 Years Ago SpaceX Nearly Failed Itself out of Existence: 'It Is a Pretty Emotional Day,' Says Elon Musk," CNBC Make It, September 29, 2017, https://www.cnbc.com/2017/09/29/elon-musk-9-years-ago-spacex-nearly-failed-itself-out-of-existence.html.

7   "What Is Experiential Learning?" Institute of Experiential Learning, accessed January 15, 2023, https://experientiallearninginstitute.org/resources/what-is-experiential-learning/.

8   Kyle Kowalski, "What Is a Talent Stack? (& How I'm Thinking about My Unique Stack)," Sloww, accessed January 15, 2023, https://www.sloww.co/talent-stack/.

9   Amy Wrzesniewski et al., "Jobs, Careers, and Callings: People's Relations to Their Work," *Journal of Research in Personality* 31, no. 1 (March 1997): 21–33, https://doi.org/10.1006/jrpe.1997.2162.

10 Cal Newport, *So Good They Can't Ignore You: Why Skills Trump Passion in the Quest for Work You Love* (New York: Grand Central, 2012).

11 Jose Gabriel Navarro, "Advertising Revenue in the U.S. 2014–2027," Statista, November 3, 2023, https://www.statista.com/statistics/236958/advertising-spending-in-the-us/.

12   Denis Diderot, *Regrets sur ma vieille robe de chambre* [Regrets on my old dressing gown] (Garnier, 1875–1877), https://www.marxists.org/reference/archive/diderot/1769/regrets.htm.

13   Diderot, *Regrets.*

14   Grant McCracken, *Culture and Consumption: New Approaches to the Symbolic Character of Consumer Goods and Activities* (Bloomington: Indiana University Press, 1990).

15   Utpal Dholakia, "Why People Who Have Less Give More," Psychology Today, November 20, 2017, https://www.psychologytoday.com/us/blog/the-science-behind-behavior/201711/why-people-who-have-less-give-more.

16   Jeff Hoyt, "1800–1990: Changes in Urban/Rural U.S. Population," Senior Living, May 20, 2022, https://www.seniorliving.org/history/1800-1990-changes-urbanrural-us-population/.

17   Mary Bellis, "History of American Agriculture," ThoughtCo, last modified August 27, 2021, https://www.thoughtco.com/history-of-american-agriculture-farm-machinery-4074385.

18   Hoyt, "1800–1990."

19   Bellis, "History of American Agriculture."

20   Elizabeth Nix, "When Did the United States Start Using Time Zones?" History, April 8, 2015, https://www.history.com/news/when-did-the-united-states-start-using-time-zones.

21   Jeff Desjardins, "Currency and the Collapse of the Roman Empire," The Money Project, February 18, 2016, https://money.visualcapitalist.com/currency-and-the-collapse-of-the-roman-empire/.

22   "The Roman Empire: A Brief History," Milwaukee Public Museum, accessed August 20, 2023, https://www.mpm.edu/research-collections/anthropology/anthropology-collections-research/mediterranean-oil-lamps/roman-empire-brief-history.

23   "Inflation and Consumer Spending," US Department of Labor, accessed February 9, 2023, https://www.dol.gov/general/topic/statistics/inflation.

24   "NASDAQ Composite Index," NASDAQ, accessed February 9, 2023, https://www.nasdaq.com/market-activity/daily-market-statistics.

25   Katie Kolchin, Justyna Podziemska, and Daniel Hadley, *2022 Capital Markets Fact Book* (New York: SIFMA, 2022), https://www.sifma.org/wp-content/uploads/2021/07/CM-Fact-Book-2022-SIFMA.pdf.

26   Jenifer Herrity, "Average Salary in the US (with Demographic Data)," Indeed, November 9, 2022, https://www.indeed.com/career-advice/pay-salary/average-salary-in-us.

27   "National Coffee Trends," National Coffee Association, accessed February 6, 2023, https://www.ncausa.org/Portals/56/PDFs/Communication/Fall-2022-media-highlights.pdf?ver=nMNTrXNtowV6CdORbLAqwg%3d%3d.

28   Pamela Vachon, "Here's How Much You'll Save Making Coffee at Home," CNET, last modified September 13, 2023, https://www.cnet.com/home/kitchen-and-household/heres-how-much-your-starbucks-habit-is-really-costing-you/.

29   "Starbucks Reports Q4 and Full Year Fiscal 2022 Results," Starbucks, November 3, 2022, https://investor.starbucks.com/press-releases/financial-releases/press-release-details/2022/Starbucks-Reports-Q4-and-Full-Year-Fiscal-2022-Results/default.aspx%2002/06/2023/.

30   Starbucks, "Reports."

31 Michael Wayland, "Key Takeaways from GM's Q4 Results and 2022 Guidance," February 2, 2022, https://www.cnbc.com/2022/02/02/general-motors-key-takeaways-from-gms-q4-results-and-2022-guidance.html.

32 "BMW Shares," BMW Group, accessed February 8, 2023, https://www.bmwgroup.com/en/investor-relations/bmw-shares.html.

33 Brian Warner, "Is It Really Possible to Retire off Royalties from One Hit Song?" December 25, 2019, https://www.celebritynetworth.com/articles/entertainment-articles/is-it-really-possible-to-retire-off-royalties-from-one-hit-song/.

34 Hugh McIntyre, "There Are Now 25 Songs That Have Been Streamed One Billion Times on Spotify," Forbes, April 2, 2019, https://www.forbes.com/sites/hughmcintyre/2019/04/02/there-are-now-25-songs-that-have-been-streamed-one-billion-times-on-spotify/?sh=2c2206c62f10.

35 "Consumer Expenditures in 2021," US Bureau of Labor Statistics, January 2023, https://www.bls.gov/opub/reports/consumer-expenditures/2021/home.htm.

36 Amarendra Bhushan Dhiraj, "These Are America's Top 10 Largest Companies by Revenue, 2019," CEOWORLD Magazine, July 26, 2019, https://ceoworld.biz/2019/07/26/these-are-americas-top-10-largest-companies-by-revenue-2019/.

37 Drew Desilver, "10 Facts about American Workers," Pew Research Center, August 29, 2019, https://www.pewresearch.org/fact-tank/2019/08/29/facts-about-american-workers/.

38 "FAQ," US Small Business Administration, last modified December 2021, https://advocacy.sba.gov/wp-content/uploads/2021/12/Small-Business-FAQ-Revised-December-2021.pdf.

39 Rosemary K. M. Sword and Philip Zimbardo, "The Importance of Our Time Perspective," Psychology Today, July 30, 2016, https://www.psychologytoday.com/us/blog/the-time-cure/201607/the-importance-our-time-perspective.

40 Jia Wei Zhang, Ryan T. Howell, and Maciej Stolarski, "Comparing Three Methods to Measure a Balanced Time Perspective: The Relationship between a Balanced Time Perspective and Subjective Well-Being," Journal of Happiness Studies 14 (2013): 169–84, https://doi.org/10.1007/s10902-012-9322-x.

41 Ashley Brantley, "Do I Have a Money Disorder? Spotting the Signs of 12 Common Financial Disorders," WellTuned, March 29, 2022, https://bcbstwelltuned.com/2022/03/29/do-i-have-a-money-disorder-spotting-the-signs-of-12-common-financial-disorders/.

42 Buster Benson, "Cognitive Bias Cheat Sheet," Medium, September 1, 2016, https://betterhumans.pub/cognitive-bias-cheat-sheet-55a472476b18.

43 Jon Street, "These Activities You May Do Regularly Pose Greater Risk of Death than Skydiving," Blaze Media, April 2, 2015, https://www.theblaze.com/news/2015/04/02/study-finds-these-activities-you-may-do-regularly-pose-greater-risk-of-death-than-skydiving.

44 Traffic Safety Facts 2019 (Washington, DC: National Highway Traffic Administration, 2021), https://crashstats.nhtsa.dot.gov/Api/Public/ViewPublication/813141.

45 Muhammad Ishfaq et al., "Cognitive Bias and the Extraversion Personality Shaping the Behavior of Investors," Frontiers in Psychology 11 (October 2020), https://doi.org/10.3389/fpsyg.2020.556506.

46 Stephen Johnson, "Time Is 'Elastic': Why Time Passes Faster atop a Mountain than at Sea Level," Big Think, December 31, 2019, https://bigthink.com/hard-science/time-perception/.

47 Scripps Howard News Service, "Time Does Fly as We Get Older," Chicago Tribune, last modified August 9, 2021, https://www.chicagotribune.com/news/ct-xpm-1994-02-06-9402060210-story.html.

48 "China's Leader Thinks in Terms of 100-Year Increments While U.S. Yardstick Is 140 Characters," MarketWatch, April 29, 2017, https://www.marketwatch.com/story/chinas-leader-thinks-in-terms-of-100-year-increments-while-us-yardstick-is-140-characters-2017-04-28.

49 Miguel Jiménez, "The Future as a Perception of Time and Context," LinkedIn, March 3, 2021, https://www.linkedin.com/pulse/future-perception-time-context-miguel-jim%C3%A9nez/.

50 Carlo Rovelli, *The Order of Time* (New York: Riverhead, 2018), 97, Kindle.

51 Kim Eckart, "How Long Can a Person Live? The 21st Century May See a Record-Breaker," University of Washington, July 1, 2021, https://www.washington.edu/news/2021/07/01/how-long-can-a-person-live-the-21st-century-may-see-a-record-breaker/.

52 Rachelle Feiler and Dana Tomonari, "Stages of Growth Child Development," Stateuniversity.com, accessed February 20, 2023, https://education.stateuniversity.com/pages/1826/Child-Development-Stages-Growth.html; "Money Smart for Young People," FDIC, August 22, 2022, https://www.fdic.gov/resources/consumers/money-smart/teach-money-smart/money-smart-for-young-people/index.html#parents.

53 Miriam Allred, "Teen Spending Habits in 2022," Lexington Law, accessed February 20, 2023, https://www.lexingtonlaw.com/blog/credit-cards/teen-spending-habits.html.

54 *2022 Survey of the States* (New York: Council for Economic Education, 2022), https://www.councilforeconed.org/wp-content/uploads/2022/03/2022-SURVEY-OF-THE-STATES.pdf.

55 *Bridging the Financial Literacy Gap: Empowering Teachers to Support the Next Generation* (New York: PwC, 2016), https://www.pwc.com/us/en/about-us/corporate-responsibility/assets/pwc-financial-education-report.pdf.

56 Connor Harris, *The Earning Curve: Variability and Overlap in Labor-Market Outcomes by Education Level* (New York: Manhattan Institute, 2020), https://files.eric.ed.gov/fulltext/ED604364.pdf.

57 Preston Cooper, "New York Fed Highlights Underemployment among College Graduates," Forbes, July 13, 2017, https://www.forbes.com/sites/prestoncooper2/2017/07/13/new-york-fed-highlights-underemployment-among-college-graduates/?sh=324c530e40d8.

58 PwC, "Will Robots Steal Our Jobs? The Potential Impact of Automation on the UK and Other Major Economies," UK Economic Outlook, March 2017, https://www.pwc.co.uk/economic-services/ukeo/pwcukeo-section-4-automation-march-2017-v2.pdf.

59 Carl Benedikt Frey and Michael A. Osborne, "The Future of Employment: How Susceptible Are Jobs to Computerisation?" (working paper, Oxford Martin Programme on Technology and Employment, University of Oxford, 2013), https://www.oxfordmartin.ox.ac.uk/downloads/academic/future-of-employment.pdf.

60 Tim Stobierski, "Average Salary by Education Level," Northeastern University, June 2, 2020, https://www.northeastern.edu/bachelors-completion/news/average-salary-by-education-level/.

61 "Trends in College Pricing 2022," CollegeBoard, October 2022, https://research.collegeboard.org/media/pdf/trends-college-pricing-presentation-2022.pdf.

62 Ben Luthi, "How Much Does It Cost to Get a Master's Degree?" Experian, April 18, 2022, https://www.experian.com/blogs/ask-experian/how-much-does-it-cost-to-get-masters-degree/.

63 Gretchen Livingston, "U.S. Women Are Postponing Motherhood, but Not as Much as Those in Most Other Developed Nations," Pew Research Center, June 28, 2018, https://www.pewresearch.org/short-reads/2018/06/28/u-s-women-are-postponing-motherhood-but-not-as-much-as-those-in-most-other-developed-nations/; Megan Thielking, "The Average Dad in the U.S. Is Getting Older," STAT, August 30, 2017, https://www.statnews.com/2017/08/30/dads-getting-older/.

64 Esther Lee, "This Is the Average Age of Marriage in the U.S.," The Knot, April 17, 2023, https://www.theknot.com/content/average-age-of-marriage.

65 Stefan Lembo Stolba, "Average Age to Buy a House," Experian, December 15, 2020, https://www.experian.com/blogs/ask-experian/research/average-age-to-buy-a-house/.

66 Wendy Wang and Brad Wilcox, *The Power of the Success Sequence for Disadvantaged Young Adults* (American Enterprise Institute and the Institute for Family Studies, 2022), https://ifstudies.org/ifs-admin/resources/reports/successsequencedisadvantagedya-final.pdf.

67 "The Success Sequence: A Proven Path to the American Dream," Institute for Family Studies, accessed February 25, 2023, https://ifstudies.org/success-sequence.

68 Johanna Maleh and Tiffany Bosley, "Disability and Death Probability Tables for Insured Workers Born in 2000," Social Security Administration, June 2020, https://www.ssa.gov/oact/NOTES/ran6/an2020-6.pdf.

69 Hal Shorey, "The Keys to Rewarding Relationships: Secure Attachment," Psychology Today, February 12, 2015, https://www.psychologytoday.com/ca/blog/the-freedom-change/201502/the-keys-rewarding-relationships-secure-attachment.

70 Emerging Technology from the arXivarchive, "Your Brain Limits You to Just Five BFFs," *MIT Technology Review*, April 29, 2016, https://www.technologyreview.com/2016/04/29/160438/your-brain-limits-you-to-just-five-bffs/.

71 JoNell Strough, "Age Differences in Reported Social Networks and Well-Being," *Psychology and Aging* 35, no. 2 (2019): 159–68, https://doi.org/10.1037/pag0000415.

72 William J. Chopik, "Associations among Relational Values, Support, Health, and Well-Being across the Adult Lifespan," *Journal of the International Association for Relationship Research* 24, no. 2 (June 2017): 408–22, https://doi.org/10.1111/pere.12187.

73 "Loneliness and Social Isolation—Tips for Staying Connected," NIH National Institute on Aging, January 14, 2021, https://www.nia.nih.gov/health/loneliness-and-social-isolation/loneliness-and-social-isolation-tips-staying-connected.

74 Jeffrey A. Hall, "How Many Hours Does It Take to Make a Friend?" *Journal of Social and Personal Relationships* 36, no. 4 (March 15, 2018), https://doi.org/10.1177/0265407518761225.

75 Dan Buettner, "How to Live to Be 100+," TED-Ed, April 17, 2013, video, 19:39, https://www.youtube.com/watch?v=ff4oYiMmVkU.

76 Marc Winn, "What Is Your Ikigai?" The View Inside Me, May 14, 2014, https://theviewinside.me/what-is-your-ikigai/.

77 Wrzesniewski et al., "Jobs, Careers, and Callings."

78 Don Miguel Ruiz, *The Four Agreements: A Practical Guide to Personal Freedom* (San Rafael, CA: Amber-Allen, 1997).

79 Mihaly Csikszentmihalyi, *Flow: The Psychology of Optimal Experience* (New York: Harper Perennial, 1991).

80 "What Is the Social Proof Theory?" Psychology Notes HQ, March 10, 2018, https://www.psychologynoteshq.com/social-proof/.

81 S. McTours, "Affective Conditioning—The Psychology of Advertising," Event Branding and Sponsorship Development, December 17, 2013, https://sponsorshiptaken.wordpress.com/2013/12/17/affective-conditioning-the-psychology-of-advertising/.

82   Hal Koss, "How the Mere Exposure Effect Works in Marketing and Advertising," Built In, last modified January 12, 2023, https://builtin.com/marketing/mere-exposure-effect.

83   Oryna Hrydasova, "How Many Ads Do We See a Day in 2023," AdLock, May 1, 2023, accessed August 1, 2023, https://adlock.com/blog/how-many-ads-do-we-see-a-day/.

84   Suzy Welch, *10-10-10: A Life-Transforming Idea* (New York: Scribner, 2009).

85   Matthew A. Killingsworth, Daniel Kahneman, and Barbara Mellers, "Income and Emotional Well-Being: A Conflict Resolved," *PNAS* 120, no. 10 (2023): e2208661120, https://doi.org/10.1073/pnas.2208661120.

86   Margery Leveen Sher, *The Noticer's Guide to Living and Laughing: Change Your Life without Changing Your Routine* (Did Ya Notice?, 2014).

87   Charlotte Wold, "The Number of Millionaires Continues to Increase," Investopedia, last modified January 23, 2022, https://www.investopedia.com/news/number-millionaires-continues-increase/.

88   Vishesh Raisinghani, "This Janitor in Vermont Amassed an $8M Fortune without Anyone around Him Knowing," Moneywise, August 28, 2023, https://moneywise.com/investing/investing-basics/how-a-janitor-became-a-millionaire.

89   Compound Staff, "The Amazing Compound Interest Story of Grace Groner," Compound Daily, last updated January 3, 2024, https://compounddaily.org/the-amazing-compound-interest-story-of-grace-groner/.

90   Tim Urban, "The Tail End," Wait But Why, December 11, 2015, https://waitbutwhy.com/2015/12/the-tail-end.html.

91   Murray Coleman, "Dalbar QAIB 2023: Investors Are Still Their Own Worst Enemies," Index Fund Advisors, April 3, 2023, https://www.ifa.com/articles/dalbar_2016_qaib_investors_still_their_worst_enemy.

92   Kristen Fuller, "Why It's So Important for Couples to Talk about Their Values," Psychology Today, August 9, 2021, https://www.psychologytoday.com/us/blog/happiness-is-state-mind/202108/why-its-so-important-couples-talk-about-their-values.

93   Mark A. Brackett, Rebecca M. Warner, and Jennifer S. Bosco, "Emotional Intelligence and Relationship Quality among Couples," *Personal Relationships* 12, no. 2 (June 2005): 197–212, https://doi.org/10.1111/j.1350-4126.2005.00111.x.

94   Michael D. Botwin, David M. Buss, and Todd K. Shackelford, "Personality and Mate Preferences: Five Factors in Mate Selection and Marital Satisfaction," *Journal of Personality* 65, no. 1 (March 1997): 107–36, https://doi.org/10.1111/j.1467-6494.1997.tb00531.x.

95   Nathaniel M. Lambert and Frank D Fincham, "Expressing Gratitude to a Partner Leads to More Relationship Maintenance Behavior," *Emotion* 11, no. 1 (2011): 52–60, https://doi.org/10.1037/a0021557.

96   "Census Bureau Releases New Estimates on America's Families and Living Arrangements," United States Census Bureau, November 17, 2022, https://www.census.gov/newsroom/press-releases/2022/americas-families-and-living-arrangements.html.

97   "Period Life Table, 2020, as Used in the 2023 Trustees Report," Social Security Administration, accessed April 30, 2023, https://www.ssa.gov/oact/STATS/table4c6.html.

98   "2023 National Population Projections Tables: Main Series," United States Census Bureau, last modified October 31, 2023, https://www.census.gov/data/tables/2023/demo/popproj/2023-summary-tables.html.

99   Anne Tergesen, "Is 100 the New Life Expectancy for People Born in the 21st Century?" *Wall Street Journal*, April 16, 2020, https://www.wsj.com/articles/is-100-the-new-life-expectancy-for-people-born-in-the-21st-century-11587041951.

100 Armin Garmany, Satsuki Yamada, and Andre Terzic, "Longevity Leap: Mind the Healthspan Gap," *Regenerative Medicine* 6, no. 57 (2021), https://doi.org/10.1038/s41536-021-00169-5.

101 Julianne Holt-Lunstad et al., "Loneliness and Social Isolation as Risk Factors for Mortality: A Meta-analytic Review," *Perspectives on Psychological Science* 10, no. 2 (2015): 227–37, https://doi.org/10.1177/1745691614568352.

102 Steven Moore et al., "Leisure Time Physical Activity of Moderate to Vigorous Intensity and Mortality: A Large Pooled Cohort Analysis," *PLOS Medicine* (November 6, 2012), https://doi.org/10.1371/journal.pmed.1001335.

103 Michael Valenzuela and Perminder Sachdev, "Brain Reserve and Dementia: A Systematic Review," *Psychological Medicine* 36, no. 4 (2006): 441–54, https://doi.org/10.1017/S0033291705006264.

104 Francesco P. Cappuccio et al., "Meta-analysis of Short Sleep Duration and Obesity in Children and Adults," *Sleep* 31, no. 5 (May 2008): 619–26, https://doi.org/10.1093/sleep/31.5.619.

105 Madhav Goyal et al., "Meditation Programs for Psychological Stress and Well-Being," *JAMA Internal Medicine* 174, no. 3 (2014): 357–68, https://doi.org/10.1001/jamainternmed.2013.13018.

106 Mo Wang and Junqi Shi, "Psychological Research on Retirement," *Annual Review of Psychology* 65 (2014): 209–33, https://www.annualreviews.org/doi/pdf/10.1146/annurev-psych-010213-115131.

107 Chris Farrell, *Purpose and a Paycheck: Finding Meaning, Money, and Happiness in the Second Half of Life* (New York: AMACOM, 2019).

108 "Aging in Place: Growing Older at Home," NIH National Institute on Aging, last updated October 12, 2023, https://www.nia.nih.gov/health/aging-place-growing-older-home.

109 "Fact Sheet: Social Security," Social Security Administration, accessed May 7, 2023, https://www.ssa.gov/news/press/factsheets/basicfact-alt.pdf.

110 David Cancel, "Charlie Munger and Warren Buffett Use This Mental Model to Stay Focused on Their Strengths," Inc., May 30, 2019, https://www.inc.com/david-cancel/charlie-munger-warren-buffett-use-this-mental-model-to-stay-focused-on-their-strengths.html.

111 "Elon Musk: A Framework for Thinking," *Farnan Street* (blog), accessed May 8, 2023, https://fs.blog/elon-musk-framework-thinking/.

112 Prasad Kaipa, "Steve Jobs and the Art of Mental Model Innovation," *Ivey Business Journal*, May/June 2012, https://iveybusinessjournal.com/publication/steve-jobs-and-the-art-of-mental-model-innovation/.

113 Based on a classic Brazilian story, probably also present in other cultures. See Paul Coelho, "The Fisherman and the Businessman," *Stories & Reflections* (blog), September 4, 2015, https://paulocoelhoblog.com/2015/09/04/the-fisherman-and-the-businessman/.